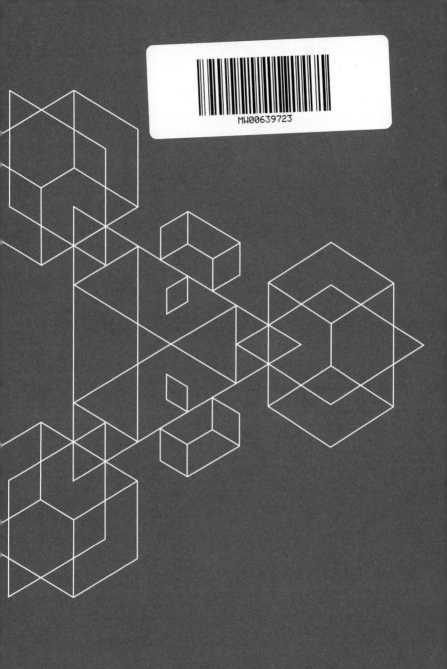

"The winners in this next phase of business evolution will be what Elliott Parker dubs 'optimistic contrarians'—and big rewards will accrue to those who are bold enough to bet on ideas that don't fit conventional wisdom. His book is full of actionable insights and enlightening examples from recent (and also ancient) history. It's a great guide to navigating what comes next."

—SCOTT KIRSNER, CEO and cofounder, InnoLead

"*The Illusion of Innovation* provides a fascinating, insightful, and interdisciplinary look at why large organizations struggle to innovate, and what they need to do if they want to redefine their industry."

—GAUTAM MUKUNDA, Author of *Indispensable* and *Picking Presidents*

"An exhilarating read that highlights the opportunity for radical change through deliberate inefficiency—arguing persuasively that it's time for organizations to find the courage to embrace the 'weird' and start anew."

—KENNETH STANLEY, Computer scientist, entrepreneur, and author of *Why Greatness Cannot Be Planned*

"Elliott delivers a masterclass on how venture building can be leveraged by corporations to foster entrepreneurial thinking and drive transformative change."

—SCOTT DORSEY, Managing partner, High Alpha

"Elliott does a masterful job breaking down what so many know but are afraid to say—the quest for safety and security puts companies at more risk than they can imagine because it makes them resistant, and even unable, to change. By busting the illusion of innovation, Elliott shows us a path forward, one that leads to resilient and enduring organizations."

—ROBYN BOLTON, Founder of innovation consultancy MileZero

"Elliott provides a thoughtful exploration of how enterprises can effectively address critical challenges in both business and society through experimentation. This is a must-read for aspiring entrepreneurs and seasoned leaders alike."

—TATE STOCK, Founder and CEO, Chirp

"*The Illusion of Innovation* provides a refreshingly honest perspective on corporate innovation, complete with an intuitive framework for implementation and supported through exhilarating examples and personal accounts."

—MATT RUBIN, Founder and CEO, True Essence Foods

the illusion of innovation

the illusion of innovation

ESCAPE "EFFICIENCY" AND UNLEASH RADICAL PROGRESS

elliott parker

IDEAPRESS
PUBLISHING

WASHINGTON, DC

IDEAPRESS
PUBLISHING

Printed in the United States

Ideapress Publishing | www.ideapresspublishing.com

All trademarks are the property of their respective companies.

Cover Design: Faceout Studio, Jeff Miller with Lauren Kellum
Interior Design: Jessica Angerstein

Cataloging-in-Publication Data is on file with the Library of Congress.

Hardcover ISBN: 978-1-64687-154-4

Special Sales
Ideapress books are available at a special discount for bulk purchases for sales promotions and premiums, or for use in corporate training programs. Special editions, including personalized covers, custom forewords, corporate imprints, and bonus content are also available.

1 2 3 4 5 6 7 8 9 10

This book is dedicated to the builders, to the entrepreneurs, to those working to create a better future. We need more people who are willing to take on the risk of experimentation, and we need more of them to succeed.

Contents

I can point out to you Roman farmers in the Sabine country, friends and neighbors of mine, who are scarcely ever absent from the field while the more important operations of husbandry, as sowing, reaping, and storing the crops, are going on. Although this interest of theirs is less remarkable in the case of annual crops—for no one is so old as to think that he cannot live one more year—yet these same men labor at things which they know will not profit them in the least.

He plants the trees to serve another age, as our Caecilius Statius says in his *Young Comrades.*

—*Cicero: De Senectute De Amicitia De Divinatione,*
as translated by William Armistead Falconer

Introduction

How to use this book.

For the last twenty-five years, I have worked with dozens of Fortune 500 companies to address the challenges of the innovator's dilemma that Clayton Christensen described. Through that work, I have concluded that most of the tools large organizations rely on to innovate do not produce the change they seek and need.

Innovation efforts pursued inside corporations too often look like theater—people acting busy doing *something* so executives can explain to the board and investors that innovation is definitely, without a doubt, a top priority. But when reviewed after the fact, most of the effort produces little impact. It is too often "sound and fury, signifying nothing." In many cases, this type of investment in innovation theater is actually value destructive, not neutral in its effect: organizations would be better off doing nothing (or actively accepting and managing their decline) instead of pretending to innovate—instead of engaging in an *illusion of innovation*.

Large companies and other institutions are better managed than ever before, but ironically, they're less capable of dealing with important challenges. They're too often focused on efficiency instead of resiliency. They're optimized for safety, predictability, and maintenance of what already exists. Their focus on capital efficiency is a deadly trap that creates fragility, not progress. As a result, many large companies are not prepared to face the future, and many are in more peril than they seem, even if the executive teams don't yet realize it. Advances in technology, communications, and finance are making it easier for small teams and individuals to disrupt the status quo. We need scaled organizations to thrive because they can solve important problems that small teams cannot. This book explains why innovation naturally emerges from deliberate inefficiency and how large corporations can harness the power of systematic experimentation to thrive in the face of an unknown future.

The hard truth is there is no formula for innovation success because every innovation is new and every organization unique. The only reliable pattern is that inspiration often comes from unexpected places. Successful innovators think about business from first principles instead of as an opportunity to apply formulas. If only there were reliable formulas!

Biographies and history books are more likely to teach first principles and to generate more ideas about what to do differently than a typical business case study. Most business practitioners would learn more about strategy from understanding Lord Nelson's actions at Trafalgar than the specifics of any challenges General Electric once faced in its financial services business. There is more enduring truth and light outside of the narrow subject of business than within it. There is much to understand from science, history, biology, and adventure that can be applied to the way organizations work to solve important problems. In actuality, creativity results from collisions, from taking an idea from one context and applying it to another. And often, the further you look outside your immediate context, the more likely your mind is to be stretched to find creative solutions.

My book is designed to take you on a journey to some faraway places to spark new and creative thoughts, generate collisions, and establish mental connections. The best innovations lead to more innovations; I hope in that sense this book is innovative for you.

The Illusion of Innovation is designed to make you question received ideas and to rethink your approach to innovation from scratch. If you're looking for a practical, how-to guide for making innovation more tangible inside of large organizations, start with this book. It will inspire you to see things differently, or to seek to do so, and to then take the action necessary to make things better. The book will rely on enduring principles, drawing from examples of the history of invention and creativity, and include a few business stories when relevant.

My aspiration is that this book will be as useful to a reader one hundred years from now as it is to a reader today. My goal in writing it is to produce a resource for those who want scaled organizations to be more effective and who are in search of a language they can use to persuade those around them to also want more change. We need our scaled institutions—our businesses, governments, universities, and churches—to be more effective at solving big problems. We need more people who are courageous enough to pursue change and to build; that is the only way this amazing world we live in will become even better.

This book is the fruit of close collaboration with many corporate executives, startup entrepreneurs, and changemakers over several years. My hope is that it will contribute to a serious conversation about the role that small teams—often embodied in startups—should play in the innovation ecosystem and how corporations can better leverage the learning abilities of startups to drive innovation and resilience. For many corporations, deep and deliberate engagement with startups will be the only way to realize the transformation they seek and regain a competency for innovation that has been lost. We have massive problems yet to be solved, and we need our corporations and other large institutions to be effective at addressing them.

Part One:

THE ILLUSION OF INNOVATION

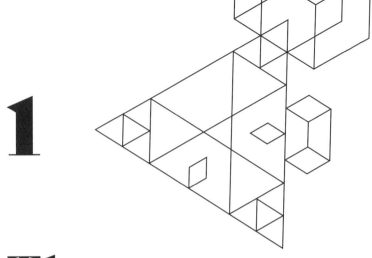

1

The capitalist's dilemma:

Gerald Shur, Clayton Christensen, and the paradox of safety

In an environment of rapid change, what feels safe is counterintuitively risky.

More people should know about Gerald Shur. When Gerald died in 2020, the *Washington Post* ran a lengthy obituary on him. Gerald was the founder of the Federal Witness Protection Program.

Gerald met his first mobster when he was only fifteen years old. The mobster was the bodyguard for a racketeer seeking to intimidate Gerald's father, a dressmaker in New York City. Gerald grew up with an inherited and well-earned hatred of the mob. When he left home he studied law, and as a young lawyer, began working for the Justice Department, where Attorney General Robert Kennedy was on a mission to stamp out organized crime. Gerald quickly realized the only way to take down the leaders of the mob was to protect insiders who testified against them. So, Gerald created the Federal Witness Protection Program to hide witnesses whose lives are in danger and provide them with new identities to prevent pursuers from tracking them down.

Since 1971, the Federal Witness Protection Program has provided security for over 8,600 witnesses and 9,900 family members. The program has been credited with helping secure thousands of convictions, including in major criminal cases.

While he was running the program, it is said that no witness got protection without Gerald's personal attention. He wrote the program's rules, shaped the program around his own philosophical views, and guided it with an iron hand.[1] He personally created false backgrounds, including employment and school records, arranged secret weddings, and organized fake funerals. He once persuaded corporate executives to hire a former hit man as a delivery driver. He arranged for people receiving protection through the program to have plastic surgery. One mobster Gerald helped protect ran for mayor of the town where he was relocated. In a strange twist, Gerald and his wife once had to enter the program themselves for a time, when a drug cartel hit man entered the United States with their names on a hit list.

The story of the Federal Witness Protection Program is a wild one. What Gerald Shur accomplished is amazing, and the impact is outsized. And for all the wild adventures and interesting side stories, the most intriguing part of the story is this: it is difficult to imagine an individual creating something like the Federal Witness Protection Program in our era and running it with the liberty Gerald Shur exercised for so many years.

The important question is: Why not? Why are our modern organizations and institutions seemingly incapable of fostering this kind of radical innovation? We are not better for it. The Federal Witness Protection Program is credited with helping topple the heads of *every* major crime family in *every* major city in the United States, sending thousands of criminals to prison.

So why don't we have more Gerald Shurs today? The short answer is that we've spent decades optimizing our institutions—our governments, our schools, our businesses—to root out the kind of variability, volatility, and risk that produce surprise successes like the Federal Witness Protection Program. Our institutions are too sterile. And this is a big problem.

We need our institutions to be effective, dynamic, and willing to try new things because we have enormous problems to solve. Most big problems can only be tackled through coordinated effort. If the organizational structures we are using to tackle big problems are less effective than they once were, what structures and ways of thinking should we use to replace them?

It is not clear whether Gerald Shur was an exception or the rule inside the Department of Justice at his time. We don't hear about many failed or successful experiments or other programs as novel as the Federal Witness Protection Program that were initiated in Gerald Shur's era, so he was likely an exception, a superhero bucking the system. We need more organizations designed to allow Gerald Shurs to flourish. Organizations are too dependent on heroic innovators like Gerald Shur, and such dependency is not a sustainable strategy. We can structurally empower and enable more Gerald Shurs, more organic experimentation, and more surprises that lead to positive change. We need messier and more vibrant companies to solve the critical problems that confront us (just as we need more capable governments and other institutions).

The reality is that we are living in a time of innovation crisis. It may not feel that way—we see the pace of innovation quickening around us. But most of that innovation is not driven by large corporations anymore. And only scaled organizations can capably address certain challenges and opportunities *at scale*: climate change, improved education, increased access to more effective healthcare, and more.

In 1997, my former colleague, the late, great Clayton Christensen, published his doctoral research in the form of a book called *The Innovator's Dilemma*.[2] In the book, Christensen explained how companies fail when executives do everything "right." By seeking to serve their best customers ever more efficiently and profitably, companies move upmarket, producing more elaborate products and leaving themselves exposed on the "low end" to disruptors who enter the market with "good enough" products to serve less-profitable customer segments. Those disruptors get a foothold in the market and, over time, move upmarket themselves, displacing incumbents. Once one learns the pattern, one cannot help but see it everywhere. Christensen's theory of disruptive innovation took the business world by storm, and "disruption" is now such a common word in business that it has all but lost the precise meaning Christensen attributed to it in his theory. If more people actually understood the nuance of the theory, they might deploy more effective strategies to deal with the challenge.

The reality is that the innovator's dilemma is a very tricky problem to solve. To address it, companies must choose to accept some capital inefficiency in their operations. The optimal amount of capital inefficiency, contrary to popular belief, is not zero. The problem is that large corporations are organized to eradicate capital inefficiency. Incentive systems from public markets down to individual compensation and promotion plans are all arranged around the premise of absolute capital efficiency, risk eradication, and security. Business schools mint thousands of MBAs every year who are trained in the doctrine of capital efficiency as the primary objective. This is what feeds and propagates the innovator's dilemma. The prioritized pursuit of capital efficiency is self-imposed tyranny, a threat to our economic future and a hindrance to progress.

Cash-rich and innovation-poor

Before he died in early 2020, Christensen was working on a new idea he called the "capitalist's dilemma." He noticed that despite an extended period of record-low interest rates, corporations that were sitting on unprecedented amounts of cash were failing to make investments in innovations that would propel more growth. Instead, most of the innovation investment was going to operational improvements to drive more capital efficiency. Investments in different types of innovation that have different effects on growth are all evaluated using the same flawed metrics, especially return on net assets (RONA), return on invested capital (ROIC), and internal rate of return (IRR). When applied to measure the success of a business, ROIC rewards executives for eliminating jobs, not creating jobs, for streamlining a manufacturing line, not making an entirely new business model or product. Christensen argued in an underrated *New York Times* opinion piece[3] (and, later, in a *Harvard Business Review* article[4]) that it is time for corporations to stop treating capital as a scarce resource.

You may be reading this and thinking, "I *wish* my company was swimming in capital!" But in aggregate, corporations have more liquid assets on their balance sheets than ever: $6.5 trillion as of early 2023, more than double the amount ten years earlier.[5] Capital is treated as a scarce resource to be hoarded and protected, a result of the pursuit of ROIC as the uber objective and measure of success.

Christensen described three types of innovation that corporations can pursue:

- *Performance-improving innovations*, or replacing old products with new models. These innovations rarely create jobs because they cannibalize existing products. When a car company sells a new model, it's usually purchased by a consumer as a substitute for another model—the consumer does not purchase both. These kinds of innovations are often called "sustaining innovations." Scaled corporations are designed and optimized for this type of innovation, and well-functioning corporations consistently produce these innovations over many decades.

- *Efficiency innovations*, or lowering operating costs. These innovations help companies sell established products to customers at lower prices. These efficiency innovations may involve a new business model—think of Walmart as an efficiency innovation in the retail industry—or they may be enhancements to a company's existing processes, like the implementation of a just-in-time production system. Efficiency innovations raise productivity (companies can do more with less) and free up cash for other uses, but they often result in eliminating jobs.

- *Empowering innovations*, or transforming products so radically that they create new classes of consumers, expand or create markets, and generate jobs for their originators and the economy. The personal computer sharply lowered the cost of access to computing power for individual consumers, and the smartphone later did the same, making computing power accessible to billions worldwide. Empowering innovations often involve some kind of technology breakthrough plus a new business model that enables access to people who were previously nonconsumers of related products. Empowering innovations often have compounding effects on their supply chain participants and in related industries. To explain the concept of empowering innovations, Christensen used the example of the Bessemer converter, which lowered the cost of steel production in the nineteenth century, revolutionizing the steel industry but also paving the way for the railroad industry and the subsequent innovations that came as a result.[6]

Financial metrics prioritize the first two types of innovation at the expense of the third. Managers and investors are trained to believe the efficient use of capital is a virtue because of its perceived scarcity. RONA, ROIC, and IRR are ratios—fractions—with a numerator and denominator that can both be manipulated to produce a better ratio. To increase RONA or ROIC, a company can generate more profit to grow the numerator and/or reduce the denominator by outsourcing more and eliminating assets from the balance sheet. IRR can be improved by generating more profit to grow the numerator or by reducing the denominator by shortening the time required to earn a return. If a company invests only in projects that pay off quickly, IRR improves.

All of this makes empowering innovations seem like poor investments in comparison with other forms of innovation that produce better efficiency metrics. Empowering innovations take years to pay off, if they pay off at all, while efficiency innovations can generate impact within a quarter or two. Empowering innovations require capital investment, while efficiency innovations free up capital in the near term. Empowering innovations require bets on new customers and markets, while efficiency innovations seem safer because they address markets and customers that already exist and are well understood.

Safety is risky

Here is the dilemma: the first two types of innovation, while necessary, do not create enduring, resilient enterprises. Only empowering innovation, repeated over time, can build an enduring, resilient business. *The pursuit of safety and efficiency at the expense of new market creation is incredibly risky over the long run.* But asking executives to act in opposition to incentives, personal interest, or short-term gains is impractical. Organizations need executives to pursue a balanced approach to all kinds of innovation, but incentive misalignment and application of incorrect metrics drive behavior that is ultimately destructive to the organization.

Doing the right thing for long-term prosperity seems at odds with what investors want, according to the metrics, tools, and timelines commonly used to guide investments. Those approaches are rooted in the quasi-mercantilist assumption that capital is scarce and performance should be assessed on how efficiently corporate executives use it. At this moment in history, capital, in aggregate, is no longer scarce, and we should be using different tools to measure success, including performance over much longer time horizons. For now, we will examine the illusion of safety in more depth.

Organizations produce the results they are designed for. Or, said differently, you can tell from the produced results what an organization is optimized to do. The question to ask of any corporation is: Is the company optimized for near-term safety and efficiency or long-term resilience? Or both? If a primary product of a company is bureaucratic deadlock, we should wonder whether such stasis is a feature or a bug of the organizational design and objectives. Political scientist Francis Fukuyama coined the term "vetocracy"[7] to describe an environment in which many more people are empowered to say no than to say yes. Corporations are—by design—vetocracies because vetocracies preserve the status quo. Chances are the organization is performing exactly as designed if decisions are deadlocked, and the design is likely optimized for maintaining the model that has worked to help the company achieve the level of success it has thus far enjoyed. Why fix what isn't broken?

If your organization does not permit people like Gerald Shur to take on risk and experiment, that is probably a feature of the organizational design, not a bug. It is a choice; it is management optimizing for safety and efficiency over long-term resilience. *People like Gerald Shur are not capital efficient.* Organizations should not rely on magic, chance, or heroes to save them. Resilient organizations not only permit people like Gerald Shur to challenge the status quo; their organizational structure, incentives, and governance attract and enable innovators to thrive.

Ultimately, every innovation is driven by a motivated and incentivized individual (or a small team of changemakers) ideally enabled, not impeded, by structure and organization.

As advertising pioneer David Ogilvy once quipped, paraphrasing G.K. Chesterton, "Committees can criticize, but they cannot create. 'Search the parks in all your cities, you'll find no statues of committees.'"[8]

One must consider the outcomes to determine what the organization is optimized to produce. Also, one must consider whether those outcomes, if they are not the explicit objectives, are the implicit objectives of the organization's design, including its governance, systems, culture, and incentives.

Large corporations are designed to be safe, to propagate the status quo and to make results predictable. It is why we see fewer Gerald Shurs than we once did; corporations are better than they used to be at optimizing for near-term results. This is why collaboration with external assets and resources in the form of nimble startups is now a more viable path for most large companies than centralization of innovation. There are very few examples of large, modern organizations that have successfully transformed their business model through internal innovation alone.

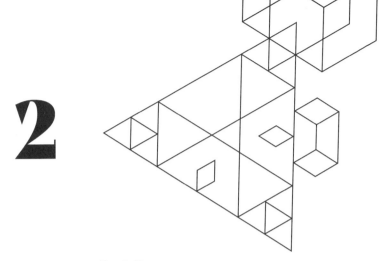

2

Resilience beats efficiency

Sustained focus on efficiency creates remarkably capable—but fragile—organizations.

I t is said that nothing online can ever really be deleted. In the case of corporate press releases, this is definitely true, and it makes for entertaining reading for those of us who care about these kinds of things. You may be interested in running the same experiment I recently ran, comparing corporate press releases from late 2019 (before COVID-19) with corporate press releases from mid-2020 (during COVID-19). The press releases reveal a fascinating contrast in priorities.

There are countless examples to choose from, but to simplify things, let's look at the announcements from a single company, Valeo, a French supplier to the automotive industry. At its apex, Valeo was an extraordinarily well-run, hyperefficient company. In late 2019, executives proudly announced they had outperformed competitors in cash generation—the metric that matters more than any other to publicly traded corporations. Even as late as February 2020, when the nature of the looming COVID-19 crisis was becoming better known, Valeo was announcing "acceleration in outperformance and cash generation in 2019," explaining how its manufacturing operations outside Hubei province in China were coming back online after a brief, virus-induced pause and noting that its supply chains were "gradually getting back in order."[1] This proclamation was dramatically premature because as the COVID-19 crisis bloomed, supply chains globally were doing anything but "getting back in order." Valeo's challenges deepened over the following year.

Press releases from mid-2020 no longer proclaimed companies' successes in driving efficiency. At the time, many executives were in fact privately lamenting the lack of resilience in their organizations, and press releases focused on reassuring nervous investors that companies were doing everything possible to cope and create resilience. In April 2020, Jacques Aschenbroich, the CEO of Valeo, told the *Financial Times* that Valeo "produced 8 million products a day before the crisis, using 3 billion components in our 191 plants." Like many other suppliers in the industry, Aschenbroich was worried that Valeo was "as weak as the weakest link in [Valeo's] supply chain."[2] He was right to be concerned: some of those links turned out to be very weak indeed.

Before proceeding further, it is worth noting what a remarkable achievement Aschenbroich, his colleagues and predecessors at Valeo, and its suppliers and customers had achieved. The company's globally optimized supply chain resulted from countless hours and careers devoted to squeezing out small efficiency improvements that, over time, created a modern wonder of the world: 191 plants coordinating their activities to deliver eight million products *every day*, on time and profitably. You can have your great pyramids, your hanging gardens of Babylon, or any other wonder of the ancient world. Valeo's supply chain was a tremendous achievement and the result of incredible human ingenuity and innovation—a quietly operating modern marvel greater than any of those ancient achievements.

Yet that hyperefficient supply chain turned out to be extraordinarily fragile when crisis came. Executives, customers, and investors learned that a single weak link could break and bring the entire supply chain down. And the automotive supply chain did indeed break down, along with Valeo's. It is unlikely to ever recover in a form that looks like it did prior to the COVID-19 crisis.

Sooner or later, crisis *always* comes. Over the long run, resilience beats efficiency and is therefore a more productive objective for scaled organizations. Innovation can (and should) be directed at both efficiency and resilience. Still, the pendulum often swings too far to efficiency, which produces organizations that are extraordinarily fragile and subject to shocks. The challenge is that our scaled organizations are optimized for the preservation of what already exists, not for building the new. They are organized for seeking efficiency, for risk eradication, for removal of variance, and for enhancement of predictability. Most of the business model innovation in large companies, to the extent it succeeds at all, drives improvements in efficiency, not resilience, and indeed not transformation. It feels safe because it promotes stability in the short run, but too much efficiency inevitably leads to failure in the long run.

This problem is at the root of plunging public confidence in the capability of large institutions, including corporations. Scaled institutions seem less capable than they once were at dealing with the big problems that confront us: pandemics, supply chain breakdowns, global climate change, access to essential resources, healthcare failures, and more. They're failing to confront the types of problems that it seems they could have solved in less time, and with less money, in the past. In so many ways, scaled organizations, including corporations, have become sclerotic in the face of challenge, unable to act competently.

Examples of this abound. A favorite: In 1995, the city of San Francisco envisioned a new two-mile bus lane on Van Ness Avenue. The bus lane was finished in 2022—twenty-seven years later—at a cost of $300 million, or about $110,000 per meter.[3] In contrast, all 1,700 miles of the Alaska Highway, connecting eastern British Columbia to Fairbanks, Alaska, were constructed in 234 days in 1942. The Alaska Highway crosses an international border and terrain that is frozen for much of the year. It was constructed for about $1,000 per meter in 2023-equivalent dollars.[4]

Of course, there are exceptions to the failures; one can find examples of successful scaled execution and even collaboration between large institutions. The Human Genome Project was a distributed, international effort to sequence the complete set of DNA in a human cell; it was initiated in 1990 and completed in 2003, ahead of schedule and under budget, resulting in a better understanding of the genetic roots of disease. Apple famously developed its first iPod and began manufacturing it at scale within the space of a few months in 2001. In 2020, SpaceX sent astronauts to the International Space Station, and it has demonstrated it can deliver payloads to space at a much lower cost than government-sponsored space programs. These exceptions, and many others like them, are worthy of study and emulation.

But on average, large organizations—including scaled corporations—seem less capable in the face of crisis—or opportunity—than they once were. The worrying paradox for the future of innovation and progress is that our institutions are better managed than ever before, but too often optimized for the wrong outcomes. They're optimized for near-term safety and predictability, for maintenance of the status quo. They are not optimized for learning.

Over the last hundred years, management science has become an established and respected field. Millions of people have obtained MBAs, studied management, or contributed to its practice. To claim that organizations are not as well run as they once were would be to suggest that all of the research and training has been counterproductive. It is much more likely that organizations are better managed than ever and that we know more about organizational design, finance, incentives, and innovation than any previous generation. Yet our institutions are more brittle.

This deliberate organizational focus on efficiency has led to a lack of resilience, and the lack of resilience is markedly obvious in scaled corporations. I have seen many examples of innovation theater across organizations, where leaders are engaged in an illusion of innovation. Chances are you likely have your own horror stories to tell. Fortunately, there are options for dealing with the challenge of innovation. There are practical—if counterintuitive—steps that large organizations can take to innovate effectively. The lessons are applicable across scaled institutions like governments, universities, and churches, but those organizational structures deserve their own separate treatment. In this book, we will focus on corporations and how to enable people to collaborate more effectively inside (and outside) of large companies to solve important problems. You'll discover strategies that can unlock transformative innovation, the elusive wellspring of enduring value creation.

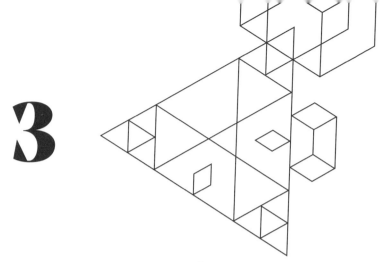

3

Embracing chaos

Thriving companies are deliberately messy, not sterile.

Years ago, I had the good fortune to visit the Sahara. The thing that surprised me the most was the stark demarcation between life and death evident at its borders. Green, vibrant plants—life—ended in a line, after which was nothing but sand as far as the eye could see. Ancient civilizations developed entire mythologies around the differences: life on one side was order, and death on the other side was chaos. For these ancient civilizations, the line between death and life, chaos and order was bright, but it was also easily crossed if one was not careful. So, they built rules around the maintenance of order, and they recognized that chaos could arrive at any time in the form of an invading horde or a natural disaster like a flood or famine to extinguish life. Chaos was evil and order was good.

Modern corporations have adopted a strikingly similar mythology.

Jack Welch, former CEO of General Electric, once proclaimed, "Variation is evil." Through management practices like Six Sigma, Welch and many others sought to eradicate risk entirely from the operations of their companies and achieve extreme efficiency, predictability, and reduction of error. Although Welch was an incredible leader and full of wisdom, in this regard he was spectacularly wrong. The idea that variation, or volatility, must be removed from companies for effective operation is unsound because it constrains ingenuity; it seeks to turn people into machines. It relies on a command-and-control system and hierarchy that does not enable flourishing and breakthrough empowering innovations. It creates an illusion of safety but squelches insight. Capital efficiency is useful, and decades of management practices are geared toward it. Companies should be efficient, but efficiency can be taken too far.

The trap of capital efficiency

The growing mountains of capital we see on corporate balance sheets are evidence of a decades-long march toward capital efficiency. Everyone knows companies need to innovate—CEOs are rightly compelled to provide evidence of innovation activity in their annual reports and speeches— yet very little of the activity seems to produce meaningful results. Far too often, innovation becomes theater, and corporate executives demonstrate uncertainty about how to invest balance sheet capital to renew and refresh their businesses.

Contrast Welch's approach with the management philosophy of Reed Hastings, founder and CEO of Netflix, who declared in a podcast interview, "Most companies overoptimize for efficiency. . . . The nonintuitive thing is that it is better to be managing chaotically if it's productive and fertile. Think of the standard model as clear, efficient, sanitary, sterile. Our model is messy, chaotic, and fertile. In the long term, fertile will beat sterile."[1]

Netflix has applied this philosophy with remarkable success, executing wholesale business model transformations since its founding: first from mailed DVDs to digital delivery, then from digital delivery to content production. Very few large corporations are able to execute a successful transformation; Netflix's acceptance of a degree of messiness (read: capital inefficiency to try new things) has enabled the company to thrive. The messiness is reinforced through incentive systems and culture, a culture that Netflix built and has maintained since its scrappy beginning. Organizations wanting to adopt a similar degree of "messiness" through process and metrics alone will find failure if culture is not part of the equation. Strong and rigid organizational designs create fewer errors, less messiness, and fewer insights.

Time will tell whether Netflix is able to maintain the messiness in the face of market pressure to adopt efficiency, particularly when new opportunities and challenges confront the business model in the form of online gaming, dynamically generated content, and globalized competition.

The trick in transformative innovation, like in certain kinds of investing, is to remember that it is the *magnitude* of correctness that matters, not the *frequency*.[2] This means you can be wrong a lot in the pursuit of transformative innovation, because on the occasion when you are right, you are likely to achieve dramatic results. Conversely, in the operation of a scaled business, the frequency of correctness matters more than the magnitude—leaders try hard to avoid anything that looks like a mistake. That tension is what makes innovation so hard.

The secret to resilience lies in creating systems that enable large-scale, big-magnitude correctness but also frequent misses. *In the face of an unknown future, the best strategy for maxi-*

mizing returns and minimizing risk is to run as many experiments as possible, at the lowest possible cost per experiment.

Radical innovation requires learning, making mistakes, and messiness. It requires a deliberate degree of capital inefficiency, an acceptance of lower-than-possible near-term RONA. Corporations are optimized for the exact opposite: execution instead of learning, predictability instead of messiness. As companies grow and scale, their operating system—the culture, incentives, governance, processes, and talent—is optimized for scaled, efficient execution, not learning. The mistake most corporations make in pursuing empowering innovation is that they try to repurpose their existing operating system—designed for efficient, scaled execution—to do something it was never designed to do: operate with a degree of inefficiency to create learning.

In practice, this looks like a corporation setting up an internal innovation team, giving them some budget, and asking them to find and develop new opportunities for the corporation to pursue. As Clayton Christensen said, "The worst place to develop a new business model is from within your existing business model."[3] These corporate innovation teams are far too often subject to the same governance systems, metrics, and processes the scaled organization relies on to operate the existing business. As a result, the innovation that does succeed ends up looking a lot like the existing business, not the transformation everyone hoped for. Gerald Shur likely would not have been successful in that kind of environment. Only superhero innovators like Gerald Shur can succeed in the face of such opposition, and rarely so. What happens when a large corporation tries to redirect the efficient machine toward the inherently inefficient activity of learning and seeking insight?

Sugar high of projections

Several years ago, scientists at a leading seed and pesticide company developed a new technology for planting sugarcane. Sugarcane is famously difficult and laborious to plant. With global demands increasing for sugar and ethanol, the company saw an opportunity to improve upon the traditional, manual process. The standard method for planting sugarcane requires a farmer to cut a piece of existing cane by hand and plant it in the ground; this involves no seeds and therefore almost no mechanization. The company's scientists developed a method for manufacturing cuttings at scale in a factory, protecting them with a chemical coating for transportation, and planting them into the ground mechanically using equipment developed in partnership with a leading tractor supplier. If successful, the method and approach promised to make the sugar industry far more efficient, lowering costs, improving yields, and increasing supply to meet global demand.

After successfully demonstrating the technology at small scale in a laboratory setting, the researchers and managers built a financial model to estimate the cost of production at scale. They determined that a factory could be built near sugar producers in a place like Brazil. Such a factory would cost as much as $100 million to construct but it *might* produce a rapid payoff in line with the internal cost of capital requirements and IRR hurdle, if everything worked according to plan.

Somewhere along the way, news leaked of the development, and market expectations were raised beyond the level of confidence of the team developing the technology. The spreadsheet model turned from a tool of exploration to an execution plan, and the company began working toward constructing a $100 million factory in Brazil. At this point, the research team began to wonder about the technology's viability at scale. The cuttings had worked very well in the lab and at a small scale, but researchers became concerned that the cuttings would not survive the time required to transport them from the factory to farms, where they would need to be planted. They suspected the shelf life of the cuttings was too short and that the cuttings would only work for farms within the immediate vicinity of the production facility.

There was a spreadsheet and a plan, and the spreadsheet showed how the investment would drive rapid results. The plan was baked into corporate forecasts and earnings projections. The team was locked in. No matter the concerns, it appeared too late for the team to back out.

Ultimately, the company built the $100 million factory, and the technology failed to work at scale, as researchers suspected. The good news is that in subsequent years, the company worked exhaustively on the shelf life problem and made improvements. Yet, the spreadsheet model the company relied upon to make the original investment decision did not depict anything close to reality.

This happens when a company applies the tools they use for execution (standard IRR forecasts, decision-making committees, planning teams, success metrics) to learning problems. In the early days, there was a tremendous amount of ambiguity surrounding the cane technology and much more to learn—the company was working in a realm of assumptions, not knowledge, but acting as if the opposite were true.

Projection models built by innovation teams operating in a realm of assumptions, not knowledge, are always wrong because prediction is not possible. In the operating business, where assumptions are low, and the level of knowledge is high, the opposite is true: financial projections can be relied upon with much more confidence. In a state of uncertainty, rapid experimentation to convert assumptions into knowledge is required. Action creates data for better decision-making. However, action taken beyond the level of confidence is more likely to result in failure at scale.

Tunnel vision

A leading aerospace and defense company makes an amazing military aircraft that can take off and land vertically like a helicopter but fly like a fixed-wing airplane by shifting the angle of its rotors once airborne. Since the aircraft was designed, executives at the company (and many aviation enthusiasts) have dreamed of a commercial version of the aircraft that would enable civilian passengers to take off and land in crowded cities, instead of at airports that are often inconveniently located far outside of cities.

In the dream scenario, a special "airport" might exist on the roof of a large downtown building. Vertical takeoff and landing (VTOL) aircraft would leave from the roof, and once airborne and above the skyscrapers, they would fly like an airplane to their big-city destination, where they'd land vertically on another similarly designed rooftop "airport."

What this company does best is design and manufacture safe, efficient aircraft. They are among the best in the world at executing their historic business model, not tinkering with new approaches to that model. And so, with permission from top executives to actively pursue exploration of the commercial viability of the VTOL aircraft, a small team began thinking through the design of the business. They hired a leading architecture firm to begin working on plans for a prototypical downtown airport, including what the lobby might look like and what kinds of restaurants and shops could be colocated in the building. They put designers to work imagining the seats on the aircraft: how they would function, what they would look like, and how they would be configured. They ran models on the cost of operation and potential cost of airfare. In short, they ran the early stages of the process they might run in their core business for a new model of an existing commercial aircraft or a partnership with an airline customer. They quickly spent millions of dollars on the early design and feasibility work.

Unfortunately, they failed to consider and test some of the most important assumptions—for example, that airlines would be interested in purchasing the aircraft to add to their fleets and that cities would allow the noise and air traffic in their downtown districts. The opportunity fell apart when the team learned no airlines were interested in purchasing the product, but by that point the company had already spent a tremendous amount of time and money. They realized too late that they were dealing with a learning challenge, but they had been treating the opportunity like it was a typical execution challenge in the core business. They had been applying the same governance, processes, incentives, and talent to something fundamentally different. They were focused on doing the things they already did best, running processes to reinforce what they already believed.

The executives at this company are some of the most capable and intelligent business leaders in the world. While this story seems rife with bad decision-making, the executives involved were operating in a system of incentives and governance that drives these kinds of outcomes; they were pushing an intransigent system to its edges. But the system wouldn't allow them to go far enough.

These kinds of corporate "sins of omission" are common. More good innovation is never pursued than is pursued incorrectly. For example, a typical multinational pharmaceutical company will spend billions of dollars yearly on product research and development (R&D), with a high degree of confidence in the implied ROI of those investment decisions. At the same time, most pharmaceutical companies spend very little capital exploring business model innovation, even though they all face existential model risk: their distribution channels are byzantine and likely unsustainable, regulatory schemes can change drastically, and wild futures exist in which consumers may be able to "print" pharmaceuticals at home. Existential risk often is found in the dark corners of the business model where no one dares look.

Permission to innovate

Early in my career, I helped lead a corporate innovation and investment team. Our job, at a high level, was to consider how to grow the core business into adjacent and transformational opportunities through investment in external startups or by building new ventures internally. Our team reported through the CFO. We were funded as an operating activity by means of a small "tax" on operating businesses that contributed funds and ideas into our funnel. Because of this, our team constantly had to fight to acquire and maintain budget, often competing against alternative uses of capital, like marketing spend, where the return on investment was well understood and the time to payback was quick. To "speak the language" of the business, we often found ourselves translating plans into IRR models so that we could argue why our projects were a better use of capital than alternatives. Our projects were not typically better as a driver of efficient returns; the opportunities we were considering were intended to create learning and future optionality for the organization, not near-term cash flow. But to win arguments, we had to make models that fit the constraints under which decisions were made so we could show what *might* happen if everything went exactly according to plan.

Investment decisions were slow and bureaucratic; because the company was based in Switzerland, our team, based in the United States, sometimes had to travel abroad to secure investment approval from top executives. The pace of our venture building and dealmaking became slower over time as decisions became harder for the organization to make and capital became more difficult to allocate to our uncertain endeavors.

It's ironic that while the CEO of the company would discuss our projects in speeches to internal audiences and public investors, we were struggling to get the support we needed to make them happen. Our work was exciting and promised a range of potential futures and growth opportunities for the company. At a certain point, our team felt like animals in a petting zoo, brought out for show but with limited ability to really do what we knew we could do best. The organizational constraints—the incentives, governance, processes, and culture—designed to protect the status quo and ensure the company moved carefully hindered our ability to experiment, learn, and succeed. Ultimately, we recommended shutting down the entire innovation operation because we were not able to have a meaningful, positive impact on the company.

Forecasting rigidity

These examples are typical of what we see across corporate innovation teams and approaches. The systems used to execute the core business efficiently, at scale, and with careful consideration are applied to challenges of learning, not execution. Despite the best intentions of all involved, the innovation efforts fail. The intention to root out errors from the system ironically ensures eventual failure.

The innovation efforts, in many cases, leave the company worse off than if nothing at all had been done. They actually destroy value, not because they do not ultimately produce meaningful results but because they provide an illusion of action when the company could instead be allocating capital and time to activities that would produce more impactful outcomes.

Scaled organizations depend on "deliberate strategy," where you set a plan and stick to it. This works well when you're operating in an environment of high knowledge and low assumptions. Deliberate strategy is optimized for execution.

Empowering innovation—often requiring a radical departure from the core business—typically requires an "emergent strategy," which allows for agility, experimentation, and pivots. Emergent strategy works best when the future is ambiguous or hard to predict. Emergent strategy is optimized for learning, which is why startups deploy it so well.

When teams are tasked with developing transformative innovations for a corporation, everything they borrow from the core business—incentive systems, core processes, governance approaches—comes with a cost. Sometimes it's worth it to associate a new corporate venture with the core brand, but teams often fail to consider the costs of borrowing from the core. Corporate hiring processes, incentive plans, and oversight committees imposed on a new venture create challenges, and leaders typically do not make those borrowing decisions deliberately.

The most dreaded sentence a corporate innovator can hear may be, "Show me your revenue and profit projections for the next year." This is an impossible request of anyone building something new, when there are more assumptions than known facts. Any sales or profitability projections at the early stage are guesses at best, yet innovation teams inside of corporations are routinely asked to perform this kind of analysis before receiving the funding they need. It's an artifact of the corporate emphasis on near-term capital efficiency; this is how capital allocation decisions are made in the core business. Executing the analysis, even if wrong, forces the team to think through the details of the opportunity, which isn't a bad thing. But models restrict the ability to pivot when they're used as planning tools and not learning tools.

The downside of this approach is that it locks teams into projections and assumptions before anyone really knows what is going to happen. Financial forecasts don't provide room for business model pivots. Every model ends up looking like a hockey stick to meet projected return requirements, with a rapid, hoped-for climb in sales and profits. When those results fail to materialize later, the venture (and usually its leaders) are deemed to have failed.

The problem is that new opportunities present learning challenges, not execution challenges. The initial focus for transformative new ventures should be on finding product-market fit through rapid experimentation. This is not a capital-efficient activity in the near term by design. In the core business, it's exactly the reverse: in a world of high knowledge and low assumptions, core business teams should be focused on execution, not learning. When execution is the challenge, building the forecast is easy (and imperative). When learning is the challenge, a reliable forecast is almost impossible. Yet companies often make decisions and fund these two different types of opportunities in the same way.

When a business unit is executing on a new opportunity that is an extension of its core business model (e.g., a new product extension), it makes sense to divert profit to fund it because the return is predictable and known. The expected ROI can be quantified and measured against the firm's cost of capital and compared against other opportunities to determine if it is worth pursuing. In these circumstances, new opportunities can and should be run in a capital-efficient manner from launch. The capital used to fund these opportunities is impatient and demands a quick return. An established restaurant chain, for example, can predict with a high degree of accuracy how the one thousandth location it builds will perform, even if in a new city, because it understands the relationship between demographics and other factors that influence demand. The organization knows when to expect a return and what that return will look like.

Conversely, when companies pursue transformative, empowering innovation, known unknowns and "unknown unknowns" prevent a reliable understanding of when a return might come or how large it might be. These kinds of opportunities require a different kind of capital, different metrics, and a different kind of calculus. For core innovations, the frequency of correctness matters more than (or at least as much as) the magnitude of correctness: companies should expect most core innovations to succeed. For transformative innovations—those opportunities that are far beyond a firm's base of knowledge—the magnitude of correctness matters more than the frequency. There will be many failures, and many lessons, but occasional spectacular successes, if done correctly. These kinds of transformative, empowering opportunities require patient capital and patient decision-makers.

Corporations can learn from the world of venture capital and venture-backed startups, where the fortress walls haven't been built and the processes of discovery and research are decentralized across many firms and investors. Payoff timelines are long, and the approach is optimized for learning, patient capital deployment, and magnitude—not frequency—of correctness. Venture capitalists are willing to be wrong a lot if they believe that when they are right, the payoff will be enormous.

Running experiments is the best way to generate data and prepare for unknown futures. In the business world, startups are a form of relatively cheap experimentation. Their operating systems—governance, processes, talent, and incentives— are optimized for rapid learning in ways that corporations' operating systems are not. By decentralizing their innovation through external startups and small teams, corporations can focus more of their innovation efforts on resilience instead of efficiency, on market creation instead of performance improvement. Corporations already know how to be efficient and how to improve performance; they are not very good at new market creation.

If the objective of innovation is resilience—not just efficiency—then innovation's success should be measured in terms of the learning and optionality it provides to the core organization. Learning can be measured by the pace at which organizational assumptions about the future are converted to knowledge. Learning occurs through experimentation, when individuals take action to test a hypothesis and the outcome is unknown beforehand. Learning involves gathering the results of experiments, making informed decisions, and evaluating the outcomes.

Is the portfolio of innovation experiments aligned with strategy, and is it sufficient to produce an adequate range of strategic options if the core business falters? If learning and optionality are the primary success metrics, then the corporation should try to avoid doing anything that would strategically constrain its new ventures. In people and in companies, growth results from actively seeking surprises, not from predictability!

The way a company approaches innovation will determine its level of resilience or fragility over time. Where a company falls on the spectrum directly impacts the company's life span and its ability to effectively engage with and impact the market.

Organizations need more messiness to achieve more insights; they need more inefficiency to enable world-changing innovators like Gerald Shur. It is that messiness, that purposeful error making, that creates resilience.

4

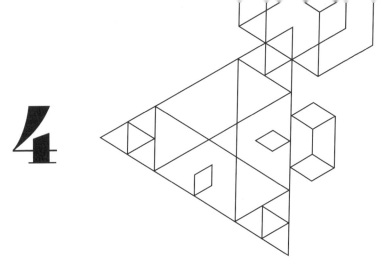

A new theory of the corporation

Corporations must reconsider their purpose, approach, and governance in a decentralized world.

At the time of its breakup by the US Justice Department in 1984, AT&T had over one million employees and a monopoly over most telephone service in the country.

It grew by centralizing expertise, assets, and resources and governing the transactions between those assets at a lower cost than could be obtained in the open market—and it earned enormous profits as a result. Although nearly all of the modern electronics we use today can trace their origin to inventions that came out of AT&T's research team at Bell Labs, the company's monopoly power probably slowed progress overall. AT&T's breakup created the opportunity for billions of dollars in annual economic efficiency gains through more rational pricing.[1]

AT&T's size at its peak may represent the zenith of the modern limited liability company and its ability to thrive in an era of centralization. That era is over, and corporations need to adapt to a world where decentralization is on the rise.

Why corporations?

In a perfectly efficient market, there would be no corporations. There would be no barriers to information, and we would each be independent, individual economic actors, coming together to transact and collaborate when needed; cooperation would be ephemeral and transactional. But corporations definitely exist! In the 1930s, economist Ronald Coase set out to understand why corporations exist, why some transactions happen in the open market, and why other transactions are managed within corporations. He won a Nobel Prize in economics for explaining that firms exist to achieve lower transaction costs, taking advantage of inefficiencies in markets to do things better inside the corporation.

A corporation can generate profit by gathering people, resources, and assets within the corporation and managing the transactions between those assets internally. This active ownership and management can enable corporations to achieve lower transaction costs than they would experience in the open market, thereby enabling them to profit. Corporations work best when they get very efficient at coordinating the assets under their control. This cooperation produces amazing things, and it has driven much of the technological progress and increase in living standards that we have seen in the world over the last century.

But the apex of the centralized corporation is likely over—at least the corporation as we've always conceived of it. The signs that this is true are abundant, but few seem to recognize that a shift has occurred. If it's now less expensive to access information, technology, or capital outside the corporation than within, the game completely changes. Why do corporations exist at all when transaction costs are now more likely to be lower outside the firm than within?

The modern limited liability corporation is one of the greatest inventions in the history of human civilization. A corporation is nothing more than an idea, a set of promises memorialized in a written contract describing how people will behave and what they will do to help each other. Its central innovation is the limited liability it provides its founders and owners; the business can fail without its shareholders facing complete ruin. This innovation allows people to take on more risk, to start things, to dream big, and to take chances.

Genesis

The modern corporation has taken shape over the last several hundred years. It is a relatively new invention, and not something that was necessarily inevitable. When people come together to collaborate in corporations, they can do amazing things, but if you were to travel back in time to Europe in the Middle Ages, you would find no corporations, no factories, and no office buildings. In fact, you wouldn't even find countries as we know them today. Governments of the time lacked the capacity to create a stable system of rules and enforcement necessary for scaled commercial enterprises. Therefore, prior to the seventeenth century, most commerce in Europe took place at the level of individual artisans and merchants, people predominantly engaging with the market through small, family-run enterprises. Guilds arose as a way for people in similar trades to cooperate and gain market power in an area, often by restricting access and information. Guilds were the precursors to chartered companies, which formed with the permission of (or on behalf of) governments to marshal the resources necessary to undertake very big tasks, much larger than an uncoordinated group of individuals could do independently. These chartered companies, like the East India Company, blurred the boundaries between pirates and governments, mobs and armies, and they had a dramatic effect on the world and modern economies as they developed in the seventeenth and eighteenth centuries. Eventually, starting roughly in the mid-1800s, through an evolution of commercial law, the modern corporation, backed by limited liability protection, came on the scene, a refinement of the models of cooperation that came before it.

Growing the pie

Prior to the rise of corporations, the dominant theory of how economies work—and how value is created and captured—was mercantilism. In a mercantilist system, a fixed amount of resources and capital are controlled by a central authority: the crown, a despot, or some other form of government. It was believed that the control helped to foster economic growth by encouraging exports and limiting imports (or, said differently, by limiting taking from others). Mercantilism argued that the sum of wealth in the world was fixed, and if the total economic pie was static, then nations (and individuals) could only become wealthier by controlling more of the pie. This meant that individuals and nations could only accumulate wealth by taking pieces of the pie from others. In a fixed-pie economy, controlling resources through a central authority, it was believed, was what made a country self-sufficient and safe—it was the only way to ensure citizens were provided for.

In 1776, Adam Smith published *The Wealth of Nations*, which explained that the economic pie was not actually fixed but could expand infinitely through specialization and co-operation. This was (and still is!) a revolutionary idea. Smith proposed the "progressive pie" economy, in which growth is possible through the increased output of goods and services and, inevitably, through innovation. Smith believed that competition between producers was essential to spur economic development and opportunity. His ideas paved the way for limited liability corporations and ultimately the rise of the individual—for a shift from piracy and violence as the primary means for individual and national wealth accumulation to cooperation, competition, and *building*.

At each stage of organizational evolution, from guilds to chartered companies to limited liability corporations, there was increased centralization and scale at the level of the organization, with more and more resources being brought within control of the corporation as a way to do big things, innovate, and profit. True, limited liability companies have rarely controlled armies like the East India Company did (although there are modern exceptions!²). On average, corporations amassed increasingly greater power over time, for a long time. In the 1950s, AT&T could gather the world's foremost experts in electronics at a place like Bell Labs and do amazing things. That kind of centralized and managed collaboration is not possible anymore, and it is important to understand why not because it has implications for the way we cooperate with others and the way we should form and manage companies. It might be said that our modern world, in which centralization, by and large, is giving way to decentralization and the power of individuals, is the culmination of Smith's ideas.

Once one understands that corporations exist to seek lower transaction costs, their structures, their governance, and the processes they use to get things done all make sense. Slow decision-making, for example, can be viewed as a feature, not a bug, for protecting the status quo, which has served the corporation well and enabled it to grow. Slow decision-making actually enhances capital efficiency by protecting and preserving assets! The inefficiency is capital efficient . . . at least in the near term.

Transaction costs and decentralization

This pattern helps explain why meaningful innovation is so hard for large corporations. I have yet to meet a corporate executive who is not frustrated by the pace and degree of change produced by his or her company's innovation efforts. For many, the sense of frustration is only growing. In the face of shrinking corporate life spans driven by disruptive innovation, everyone knows corporations need to do better, but innovation success also seems more elusive. What to do?

The old, mainstay approaches to innovation relied on the fundamental centralization premise of corporations—gather the world's experts on a topic within the corporation, incentivize them appropriately, and watch them solve important problems faster and more efficiently than the open market could. For many decades, corporations used internal R&D to create seemingly magical product and business model innovations. However, in a world where individuals and small teams have inexpensive access to information, technology, and capital that only corporations previously could claim, the old corporate approaches are no longer as effective.

Exponential improvements in computer processing speeds, increased access to ideas, and abundant capital all create lower transaction costs. They make it easier for small teams and individuals to coordinate with others to get work done, and throw into question the very reason why Coase explained that corporations exist at all. If a corporation is not actually achieving lower transaction costs through unique access to knowledge, communications, capital, or some other advantage, *it is dying*. The company's executives are *corporate hospice workers*, although most may not realize it yet. They persist in trying to innovate, with most of the innovation investment going to incremental ideas that, at best, will result in small enhancements in efficiency. At the same time, the market focuses on exponential, transformational opportunities the corporation can no longer unlock. Sustaining innovations are wonderful—most of the innovations that make our world amazing are incremental improvements over what existed before—but companies can only depend on sustaining innovations or efficiency improvements for so long. The luck and advantage eventually run out.

The limits of corporate R&D

As innovation in information technology, communications, and capital access has impacted every market, corporate executives have done their best to cope. In the beginning of the twentieth century and up through the post–World War II era, companies succeeded in driving transformational growth through technology innovation and centralized R&D, like at Bell Labs, IBM, or Xerox PARC. As more competition in technology took hold, executives turned to financial engineering—including mergers and acquisitions (M&A), private equity, and globalization—as a path to growth. General Electric was a top performer in the 1980s and 1990s, focusing on extreme operational efficiency, geographical arbitrage, and explicit financial engineering models like GE Capital.

In our current era, R&D and M&A remain the primary tools for driving innovation and growth for large companies; R&D and M&A investments are increasing each year, on average. But as primary drivers of breakthrough growth, these approaches are becoming less impactful. They are both harder to execute and less financially rewarding than they were in the past, partly because they work best in a theory of the firm that thrives on centralization. That does not mean R&D and M&A should not be an essential part of every large company's innovation toolkit—they remain essential. It just means they should not be the only tools, and expectations about their effectiveness should be adjusted down.

US firms still invest massive amounts of money in scientific and technological searches for new ideas: as much as half a trillion dollars in 2019.[3] But returns to R&D are diminishing, perhaps sharply. Over the past century, we have vastly increased the time and money invested in science, but we are producing the most important breakthroughs at a near-constant rate. On a per-dollar or per-person basis, this suggests that science is becoming far less efficient.[4]

One reason it is less effective? Many think that good ideas are getting harder to find. To keep up with the Moore's Law pace of improvement in semiconductors, for example, the microchip industry has to spend increasingly massive amounts on R&D. The number of researchers required to double chip density today is more than eighteen times larger than the number required in the early 1970s.[5]

The diminishing returns to R&D in other industries are even worse. Research productivity for the aggregate US economy has declined by a factor of 41 since the 1930s, an average decrease of more than 5 percent per year.[6] So, even as the average firm size has grown, the large firms that tend to do most R&D have become less innovative.

At the same time, companies are buying back their stock in record volumes, which can be interpreted as a sign that executives, in many cases, no longer believe in their ability to invest shareholders' money in innovation to drive market-beating returns. Repurchases reduce a company's ability to invest in innovation and other new opportunities; executives who execute buybacks may believe new opportunities are fewer, or their ability to execute on them is questionable. Between 2010 and 2019, US firms distributed $4 trillion in dividends and $6 trillion in buybacks; in total, they distributed about $4 trillion more than they raised.[7] In 2022 alone, companies listed in the S&P 500 executed nearly $1 trillion in share buybacks—a record number that was twice the amount of dividends in the same period.[8,9]

Despite record deal flow, private equity firms are struggling to deploy their trillions of dollars of "dry powder." These multiyear trends suggest that large firms are having a hard time finding meaningful projects and generating new ideas to drive returns. They are struggling to innovate in a way they once seemed capable of doing.

Acquisitions era

The larger companies get, the more they rely on acquisitions to grow and transform. However, as the average life span of companies declines because of faster cycles of innovation,[10] it is reasonable to expect the length of time over which companies can extract rewards from their acquisitions also to shrink. In 1976, there were just under 4,600 publicly traded companies in the United States. By 1996, that number had grown to over 7,300 companies. But since then, the number has plummeted to a little over 4,200. According to investor Michael Mauboussin, "There were fewer public companies in the U.S. in 2022 than there were in 1976 notwithstanding that the population in 2022 was 1.5 times that of 1976, real gross domestic product (GDP) per capita was 2.2 times higher, and the number of firms was roughly 1.5 times greater. The 'listing gap' is the difference between how many public companies are listed and an estimate of how many should be listed, given the size of the population and economy as well as listings in other countries. Researchers estimate the gap in the U.S. is 5,800 to 12,200 companies."[11] Public firms are fewer and, on average, larger, but not more innovative.

Over the last three decades, the average cost of an acquisition has roughly tripled.[12] We are seeing a trend where the number of acquisitions remains relatively flat, while valuations increase, signaling that good deals may be harder to achieve. Acquisitions are a more difficult way to unlock innovation than they once were.

Waning globalization

Globalization was a primary driver of efficiency gains for many decades, and the era of globalization is not over—yet—but many of its cost savings have already been realized. Since World War II, billions of people worldwide have moved to cities and joined the middle class. Complex supply chains proliferated, competitors merged, and companies planted operations across the globe. In many cases, for the largest firms, there is nowhere else to go, and many are now consolidating some of their far-flung operations as efficient supply chains prove fragile in the face of crisis.

With these powerful headwinds, the narrative about business over the coming decades will be one of reinvention and disaggregation of the firm. After reaching a peak of corporate and industry concentration, the decentralizing powers of disruptive innovation are changing the landscape. Many executives are still pretending, and perhaps hoping, that they can innovate like before, within the existing corporate structure. But many also worry that when the dust settles, their good intentions and expensive innovation investments will have been for nothing: just an illusion.

There are, of course, exceptions to the decentralization trend. The internet, while fostering access to information and expertise on an unprecedented scale, also centralizes power in some instances. Top internet companies achieve power law returns: the leading company in a domain wins most of the market share, and the number three and lower companies earn almost none. In the physical world, a company that is 20 percent better than its competitors might garner a slight increase in market share. For example, a restaurant in a town fifty miles away might be plainly better than the restaurant down the street from you, but that does not mean you are more likely to go there. Distance, in this example, is a powerful barrier. On the internet, however, barriers to access are few. An internet company that is 20 percent better than its competitors won't just earn 20 percent more business; it will achieve close to 100 percent market share because distribution costs are low. Most customers will choose to use the service that is best, and the pace of adoption for winners can be astounding. The internet picks sole winners in categories, and data gets centralized this way.

But even this type of aggregation is, counterintuitively, a sign of decentralization because the teams running these firms are smaller than the teams running similarly sized firms in the past. As the chart on the next page shows, the number of workers required to generate $1 million in revenue has decreased sharply over the last few decades, largely because of efficiencies from information technology. Smaller teams can do bigger things, and less centralized coordination is required than in the past. The data may be centralized, but the teams are smaller. This isn't necessarily better than how corporations organized and operated in the past, but it is markedly different.

More with Less
Workers needed at S&P 500 companies
to generate $1 million in revenue

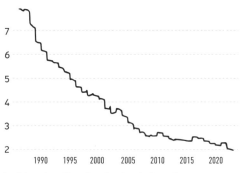

Source: Bank of America, Chart: Bradley Saacks/Semafor

Suppose our current concern with corporations is that they're ineffective in the face of change. In that case, we should also be worried about too much of the opposite: a future in which everything is intermediated by a few dozen critical corporate- and government-controlled databases. Such a scenario would undoubtedly lead to bad behavior and barriers to further innovation. An alternative scenario also exists, however, where small teams and individuals remain capable of swarming to tackle new challenges that arise, thereby rendering old centralized databases less critical or forcing databases open and transforming them into public ledgers. It is a safe bet that despite data centralization, new companies will continue to rise and fall at faster rates than before, led by smaller teams.

In the meantime, capable leaders at the largest corporations are spending billions of dollars to propagate an illusion of practical, centralized innovation. Evidence can be seen in the macroeconomic data of a significant productivity slowdown in traditional industries, which make up 70 percent of the economy; all the innovation activity does not seem to be producing lasting change.

Big companies are making serious investments in innovation, often empowering internal teams to mimic the creativity and action of more agile startups. One large financial services firm I worked with ran a two-hundred-person innovation team for more than seven years, with over $50 million invested annually. That effort never produced a single dollar of incremental revenue. A national grocery chain that operates an innovation center with more than one thousand employees set a bold goal a few years ago to invest $100 million in a single year in innovation but struggled to find meaningful ways to spend the budget effectively.

Scaled corporations need a new approach and may need to consider a redefinition of the firm itself. The micro- and macroeconomic shifts caused by advancing technology have been profound and promise to become even more meaningful in coming decades, suggesting that a new formula for a new type of organization is required: a mix of old and new, big and small, hard and soft, atoms and bits. The digital tools that changed communication- and information-based industries like media and finance are now transforming physical industries too. Although executives at most big firms understand this—every corporation seems to have a "digital transformation" strategy—many are not equipped to exploit the new opportunities internally.

The corporation as we once knew it is dying and may already be dead. But we need corporations to succeed; they provide a unique mechanism for broad cooperation that encourages risk-taking and the deployment of solutions to significant problems.

Part Two:

RECAPTURING PROGRESS

5

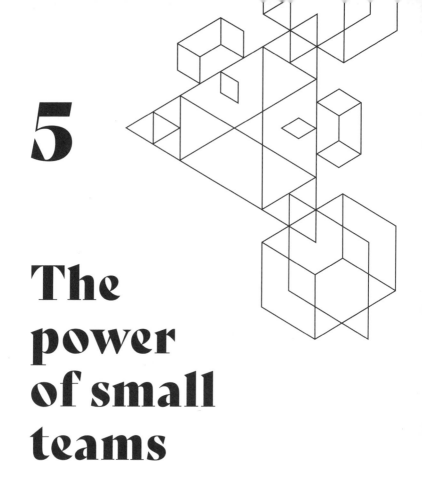

The power of small teams

A new era of decentralization is empowering small teams and individuals to disrupt traditional corporations.

At the time of its acquisition by Facebook, Instagram famously had no revenue. Yet pre-IPO Facebook paid $1 billion for the company when the price was considered a massive expense. The deal was initially ridiculed as a sign of Silicon Valley froth and overexuberance, but what seemed like a questionable move at the time was not doubted for very long, as user adoption grew swiftly and the business became an important revenue generator for Facebook, later renamed Meta. With the benefit of hindsight, the acquisition is regularly cited as one of the best deals in the history of Silicon Valley.

Years after the acquisition, emails from Facebook founder Mark Zuckerberg revealed that he thought Instagram posed a grave competitive threat to Facebook. At the time of the acquisition, Instagram was courting many potential suitors, including the investment firm Sequoia and the social media site X, formerly known as Twitter, which had offered to buy the company for between $500 and $700 million in stock.[1] Zuckerberg quickly stepped in and offered to buy the company for "double whatever [Instagram] was raising [their] round at." Kevin Systrom, founder of Instagram, countered with an offer for $2 billion. Zuckerberg whittled down the price, aiming for a target close to 1 percent of Facebook's expected IPO value of $100 billion. Systrom accepted the value, believing that Facebook's stock would rise over time, resulting in an eventual value closer to his original $2 billion asking price.

Executives at Facebook were initially shocked at the deal size. At the time, Instagram had between twenty-five and thirty million users, while Facebook had hundreds of millions. But Instagram had heavy interactions, including between consumers and businesses that were posting photos of their products in the app. Facebook executives came around on the merits of the deal and its price through Zuckerberg's persuasion, and the company then moved quickly to execute the deal.

Ironically, Systrom faced more pushback from his board than Zuckerberg faced from his board or executive team. Systrom explained to his board that the value of the purchase would go up, Facebook's scale would accelerate Instagram's growth, and in the deal, Instagram would be neutralizing what they viewed as their largest and meanest potential competitor. His board agreed, and the agreement was executed soon thereafter.

The most remarkable thing about all of this? Instagram only had thirteen employees at the time of the acquisition. Thirteen employees servicing as many as thirty million customers. Before widespread global adoption of the internet and software, that kind of leverage would have been unthinkable.

Advances in information and communication technologies have enabled faster cycles of invention and greater access to expertise and knowledge. This allows smaller teams with limited resources to do what could only have been done previously with much larger teams and greater access to capital.

Small teams can now expect more available rewards going forward. The coming century will likely be more decentralized than the last. This means that individuals will become more influential and powerful. In the past, a single executive at a company like AT&T could have had over a million employees under his supervision. However, such scaled operations are unlikely to be witnessed again. The average company will become smaller in size, as individuals (and their bots?) become more effective and powerful. Instagram's exit value per employee may be viewed one day as relatively insignificant.

Effective organizations can now be built faster and for less money than they could in the recent past. This is evident in the venture builder that I run, where we're able to launch and support more startups with the same inputs than we could even a few years ago.

Consider the illustrative math that author and investor Packy McCormick uses to demonstrate the declining cost of company creation and the unbounded potential upside of the power of smaller teams to effect change:[2] Imagine that a few decades ago a new company required one hundred people to launch and achieve market traction. Thanks to technological advances and access to capital, now those one hundred people might start ten companies instead. One company for the first ten people, and then the remaining ninety people are free to go start nine more companies. Those companies are likely able to do more advanced things, relying on the building blocks created by those who came before them.

This mental experiment is manifested in actual data. The average company size has shrunk over the last twenty-five years,[3] ultimately heading toward a limit of one person—or maybe, to be provocative, one computer. The reduction in firm size might correctly be interpreted as a sign that transaction costs are indeed lowering, as Coase explained.

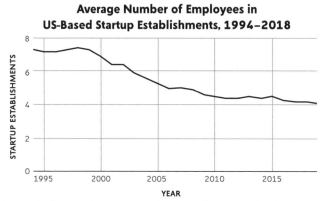

Average Number of Employees in US-Based Startup Establishments, 1994–2018

Sources: Business Employment Dynamics, Quarterly Census of Employment and Wages, and authors' calculations.

Small teams, including small teams in the form of startups, will be the changemakers. "Startups operate on the principle you need to work with other people to get stuff done, but you also need to stay small enough so that you actually can," noted investor Peter Thiel in his book *Zero to One*. "Positively defined, a startup is the largest group of people you can convince of a plan to build a different future. A new company's most important strength is new thinking. Even more important than nimbleness, small size affords space to think."[4] In the face of rapid change, clear thinking is more important than ever.

If the old model for a corporation was like a fortified medieval town, with a high wall protecting the edges and the assets safe inside, the new model is much more porous and connected. The firm's borders are disintegrating, and the big companies, investors, and startups that learn to coordinate effectively will be able to turn threats into mutually beneficial opportunities. Corporations need access to small teams that can think and act clearly in the face of massive challenges and opportunities without the baggage of feeling compelled to propagate what has worked before.

For big companies, the recipe for victory has changed from centralized, hierarchical control of owned assets to coordination of decentralized, "borrowed" assets. This change requires a rethinking of the underlying processes a company uses to run its operations, how it makes decisions, the incentives it uses to shape behavior, and even the talent it hires, retains, and promotes. Corporations are playing a different game now, and many executives don't yet know it.

Startups do it better

Nimble startups that can learn and grow quickly are poised to thrive, while traditional, scaled firms feel intense disaggregation pressure. We should expect the rise of new, more decentralized organizational models for solving problems. Startups are the source of almost all of the dynamism in our economy in the modern era.

A growing stack of innovative economic research says startups are the key to economic revival. MIT's Daron Acemoglu and colleagues estimate that young firms are about 50 percent more innovative than even R&D-focused incumbents—existing firms that spend lots on innovation. The research suggests that the economy would be better off if large firms were paid to shut down so creative talent could be unleashed to pursue fresh starts. Acemoglu and his team simulated policies that would shift financial and human capital to various types of firms to maximize innovation and macroeconomic growth. Acting as an omniscient industrial planner, they discovered that the optimal approach would be to apply a very high tax, around 70 percent, on the operations of low-productivity incumbents to encourage them to exit product lines and liberate workers. Their optimal policy "forces low-[productivity] incumbents to exit at a very high rate, reduces their R&D, and increases the R&D of high-[productivity]" firms.[5] Innovation theater is inhibiting the real thing. Corporations (and the economy broadly) would benefit from a reallocation of innovation investment from centralized R&D inside of corporations to decentralized startups.

In a related 2023 study, researchers Ufuk Akcigit from the University of Chicago and Nathan Goldschlag from the US Census Bureau revealed that large companies are squandering the innovation potential of top inventors.[6] A survey of employment and patent data showed that inventors are increasingly concentrated in large firms, and when large firms employ an inventor, that inventor's earning increases 12.6 percent while his or her innovative output declines 6 to 11 percent. This is a problem: the study showed that "the share of inventors employed by large, incumbent firms rose from 48 percent [in] 2000 to about 57 percent in 2016." Not only do inventors at large companies lower their output relative to peers employed in more entrepreneurial structures, but the quality of their output declines. Inventors at large companies produce "lower quality innovations, with fewer citations, fewer citations per application, fewer independent claims, and more self citations (e.g., more incremental)." Large companies are squashing innovation.

Acting like a startup

Over the past twenty-five years, small businesses have created 12.9 million net new jobs in the United States, accounting for two of every three jobs added to the economy.[7] With their messy and organic governance, willingness to experiment, and extreme incentives, startups are optimized for unleashing human ingenuity in ways that sterile, efficient, scaled corporations are not. We need more startups!

Many corporate executives are tempted to look at startup successes and instruct their teams to act more like a startup. For most corporations, this would be a terrible mistake—despite the many well-known successes, most startups fail. A corporation trying to act like a startup is like a high school marching band trying to play improvisational jazz: it may sound like a fun idea, but the result is chaos. Corporate strength lies in coordination, not nimbleness, and in efficiency of execution, not speed.

Large corporations must recognize that the resources they need to coordinate are now more broadly distributed than in the past and unlikely to be found or gathered internally. Similarly, centralized approaches to innovation will not work as well as they once did. There will never be another Bell Labs in terms of the ability to gather a group of top experts under one roof and profoundly influence multiple fields. The world has changed. Firms need a new approach to boost innovation in the short term and expand optionality and learning in the long term. Corporations must learn to collaborate with outside experts, small teams, and startups in this new environment if they are serious about innovation.

The new, decentralized world order requires a faster pace. Only startups with well-incentivized entrepreneurs can reimagine the existing world and deploy resources quickly enough to learn, discover new products, and coordinate talent effectively in this environment. Corporations produce incremental returns. Startups produce exponential returns—when they are successful. That is great for startups, but where does it leave big firms? The opportunity for large firms is enormous, but only if corporate executives recognize the shift and take advantage of it.

Many examples of successful innovation result from collaboration between large corporations and nimble startups, but most are still the result of acquisition. Apple's purchases of Siri (the foundation of its natural language and AI efforts) and PA Semi (which turned into its "A" microprocessors that power billions of iPhones and iPads) are examples of this. Amazon revolutionized its fulfillment centers through its purchase of Kiva Systems and its acquisition of Yap in 2011, and in 2012 it acquired Evi, which evolved into Echo and Alexa in 2014. Firms that execute their R&D through decentralized, independent startups in this way are innovating faster than those that do not. Acquisition is not the only way to collaborate, and we should expect that changing macroeconomic conditions will result in more partnerships and perhaps more corporations investing and incubating external startups from scratch to access hard-to-achieve innovation.

For incumbent firms in many industries, a more expansive reimagining of R&D, M&A, corporate venture capital, and even the boundaries of the firm is required. The path to success is to build and support fully autonomous startups that produce strategic and tactical streams of technology, talent, economic value, data, and market lessons exploitable by the large partner.

It is technology that is driving down Coaseian transaction costs, allowing this new strategy of "modular coordination": startups are cheaper and easier to launch, capital is more accessible, and expertise more abundant. In the early twentieth century, Henry Ford was right in believing the most efficient way for his company to manufacture cars was to control the entire value chain, from rubber production in South America to the manufacturing of standardized parts in Dearborn. There were no other experts to rely on, and Ford could access and control the capital required. In the twenty-first century, Ford Motor Company's production is much more modularized, depending on a vast system of closely linked suppliers.

The methods people rely on to solve problems and get work done are becoming ever more decentralized and are likely to become more autonomous. At the same time, venture capital networks are maturing, and startup ecosystems are expanding. The art and science of launching successful startups is now itself a form of expertise, with a new breed of "venture builders" like the company I run finding success in the business of quickly and systematically launching new companies. These trends are marching beyond traditional technology-heavy, "bits"-driven industries into the physical economy and world of "atoms," as software continues to "eat the world."[8]

For large firms, the tactics of startup engagement will depend on their unique nature and market position. A firm's age, industry, competitive advantage, and unique challenges will inform the best ways to engage startups through borrow, build, or buy tactics. On the spectrum of control, firms will have to decide how to adjust the dials of independence. For some scaled corporations, a complete and immediate reboot of the business model will be required. For others, learning and exploration in anticipation of a future need to transform will be enough—for now.

6

Nature abhors a hierarchy

Corporate leaders can learn from enduring natural systems, which innovate without management or objectives.

We need our planet to sustain life, and the Amazon basin plays an important role in our global weather systems and even the content of the air we breathe. Perhaps no individual ecosystem is more important to the survival of life on our planet:

- The Amazon River carries 20 percent of all the water carried by rivers worldwide, so much water that it continues flowing for up to one hundred miles into the Atlantic before mixing with salt water.[1]
- Its jungle is so dense, hot, and humid that half of its rainfall comes from the trees' transpiration.[2]
- The Amazon is so wide, and its volume so variable, that no bridges can realistically be built to cross it.

Fortunately for us, the Amazon basin is extraordinarily resilient. We must be careful, of course, but we can also rest assured knowing the Amazon probably isn't going anywhere anytime soon. There are many lessons that scaled organizations can learn about resilience from enduring ecosystems like the Amazon.

A corporate innovation leader once explained that his company was particularly good at "failing slowly and at scale." Vibrant ecosystems in nature do the opposite: they push innovation to the boundaries, to the level of mutations in individual cells or organisms, and if those mutations fail, the ecosystem is unaffected. On the other hand, if any of those mutations are successful, the ecosystem is poised to adopt the change.

Years ago, I traveled to the Peruvian Amazon with my son, an aspiring entomologist who was preparing to enter university. We journeyed to a particular sixty-square-mile portion of the jungle that has been relatively unaffected by climate swings over the eons. Other parts of the Amazon have experienced fluctuations in rain, humidity, and heat, but this particular section of the Amazon basin has remained relatively stable. It now boasts what might be the most incredible biodiversity of any location on the planet. There are more varieties of insects, birds, and monkeys in this dense area than anywhere else, which makes it an attractive place for scientists to conduct research. To date, scientists have only succeeded in naming and classifying a small portion of the insects that inhabit the area.

While my son and I were there, we worked with local guides to set up light traps for insects at night. The traps consist of a white bedsheet hung between two trees and a bright light directed at the sheet. Very quickly, insects are attracted to the light and land on the sheet. Within minutes, the entire sheet was covered in a variety of insects. My son was in heaven looking at all the insects we found, many of which we could not find in any formal classification. The variety of shapes, camouflages, colors, and appendages was remarkable. One moth variety was especially astonishing—it looked like a broken twig caught on the sheet—even when looking very closely, it was hard to believe it was a moth!

Charles Darwin's key insights about natural selection are well known. To develop his theory, Darwin gathered a massive trove of evidence, including from breeders of roses, wheat, and dogs; from fossil records of worms, fish, and mammals; and from the anatomy of living organisms. He famously studied species from remote places like the Galapagos Islands, where he found many examples of creatures whose ancestors were transported by wind or sea and freed from competition to develop into new forms. Ever since, naturalists have continued to gather examples of evolutionary biology, sometimes much closer to home than the Galapagos.

The case of the peppered moth *Biston betularia* is a good example (and now a famous one) of evolution in action. The peppered moth is not famous for how it stands out, but rather for how it fits in. It is unremarkable and easy to miss for that reason, but its ability to blend in is what makes it an amazing creature. The pattern and coloration of black and white speckles on its gray wings is ideal camouflage for lichen-covered tree trunks in its natural English habitat. Moths with speckled wings match a tree's texture and coloring and are much harder for predatory birds to spot than their more conspicuous competition. Scientists have run experiments where they pin moths to a tree and monitor how often they get eaten by birds; these mad scientist–like experiments show conclusively that dark varieties of these speckled moths on trees are eaten more often than light ones.[3]

Dark moths arise from occasional DNA mutations that impact a gene affecting wing color. These mutations create a new form of the gene, which turns the wing black and makes it stand out to predators. During the Industrial Revolution, buildings and trees were more likely to be covered in dark soot than they had been in centuries prior. The tables turned: the dark moths were advantaged because of their coloring, while the lighter moths were more easily revealed against a dark backdrop. As air pollution increased and covered more trees in soot, dark moths spread, and the number of lighter moths decreased, until dark moths became the prevalent form in more polluted areas.

Within a half century, dark moths completely replaced light moths in the industrial town of Manchester. A well-known polymath of the time, J. B. S. Haldane, developed a formula to calculate how much more likely light-colored moths were to be eaten by a bird than a dark moth. He determined that the answer was about 30 percent, a difference great enough to transform an entire population's wing color within a human life span.[4]

The moth species demonstrated extraordinary resilience, obtained not through careful planning, coordination, and execution, but through random mutations at the level of individual organisms. It turns out that good things can happen in the system when evolution is free to explore a wide range of possibilities.

Resilience is the ability of a system to absorb disturbance and still retain its basic function and structure. Nassim Nicholas Taleb described an even higher aspiration in his book, *Antifragile*, in which he showed how systems can actually emerge from shocks stronger than before, if they are organized to do so. The example he gives is of a box marked "fragile": if you shake the box, the contents will likely be destroyed. In a box marked "antifragile," the contents would emerge from the shaking stronger than if they had been left alone. We should strive to build resilient corporations, even antifragile ones, because they will be better equipped to solve the big problems facing humanity.

Resilience is developed and maintained through learning, optionality, and redundancy. Resilience is never the result of top-down, hierarchical management. It is always the result of organic, messy experimentation. Resilience requires a certain degree of inefficiency, randomness, and exploration.

Messiness as advantage

Fragility, on the other hand, results from too much focus on efficiency and is often the output of a top-down, hierarchical organizational structure over time. Companies that are over optimized for a specific moment in time or a limited set of market conditions are fragile. They might function very well in a certain context but will struggle greatly when the context shifts. Like a monoculture facing threats from disease or pollution in an ecosystem, a fragile system can find itself in mortal peril when there's a deviation from the current, steady state. And there are always deviations! It is a question of when, not if. A simple change in the market environment (e.g., a new competitor, a change in the cost of capital) can kill a fragile company. A company that encourages "monoculture" with rigid governance will miss opportunities for mutation and is choosing a strategy that will ultimately lead to fragility and insolvency.

Companies that want to limit fragility and increase their resilience must develop a means for rapid, organic, and "cheap" experimentation. Companies that want to limit fragility need to find ways to circumvent the vetocracy that exists to help the scaled organization combat changes that threaten the status quo. Experimentation has to move beyond optimization and efficiency into the realm of new market creation and transformation; novelty is an admirable goal of experimentation and an end in itself for the learning it provides, not simply a means to an end.

Resilient companies can withstand failure, crises, and changes in context and turn these dangers into opportunities to gather information, learn, and become smarter. Resilient companies learn how to take on and manage risks and how to embrace an optimal amount of volatility. Resilient companies push innovation and experimentation to the boundaries, to the corporate equivalent of individual cells and organisms, where failure costs little but success drives change. Rather than fail slowly and at scale, they learn quickly and through the cumulative collection of many small insights.

Executives determine whether their companies are optimized for fragility or resilience, and how the company pursues innovation is the primary determinant in the choice.

Over many generations of mutation, natural selection produces an astonishing amount of variation. What's remarkable is that the process is unguided. It's a random walk: no plans, no objectives, no goals. Success is the natural byproduct of learning.

Some might argue the objective of evolution is to find organisms capable of surviving and reproducing. But if that were true, there would not be so much divergence, and evolution would have perhaps stopped with single-celled organisms, which are extraordinarily resilient and prolific. The abundance of diverse species suggests that something else is going on. Survival and reproduction should be viewed as constraints, not objectives.

Through experimentation, evolution accumulates different ways to survive and reproduce. When simpler approaches are exhausted, evolution gradually uncovers more complex forms of life. These later forms of life are not necessarily improvements over earlier forms of life but the next steps reachable from where the ecosystem last stood.

The Amazon has a remarkable ability to gather knowledge on diverse ways of surviving and reproducing, making it highly resilient. Regardless of the challenges it faces, the Amazon is likely to sustain life for a long time. Similar to the peppered moths studied by Haldane, the Amazon has developed an innovation strategy that fosters long-term resilience.

The lessons

What lessons can we learn from resilient ecosystems about how large corporations can better adapt and thrive?

1. **There are no objectives**
   Evolution is not a planned, top-down, command-and-control kind of endeavor. It is a random walk. It

is natural, unstructured, messy, and chaotic. Limited resources act as constraints that drive selection, but otherwise there is no grand vision at work. The goal of evolution in the Amazon is not to create some kind of superorganism. Rather, evolution is simply the accumulation of knowledge about new possibilities. If it were objective driven, it would not be so prolific. Contrast this with innovation inside of organizations, which is top-down, planned, objective driven, and typically far from prolific. So often corporate innovation is pursued with the express goal of creating a new superorganism—a stronger and reimagined business model—rather than simply exploring what's possible, and the objective is never reached.

2. **Experimentation happens at the margins**

Experiments, in the form of mutations, are pushed out to the level of individual cells and organisms within the ecosystem. When those mutations fail the fitness test, it is unfortunate for the cell or organism involved. But the ecosystem is fine, and perhaps even stronger. When those mutations succeed, the ecosystem is poised to adopt them and let them flourish. Furthermore, experimentation is typically siloed—mutations are not broadly communicated at first; they are not shared. *This lack of communication is a feature in innovative systems, not a bug.* (Jeff Bezos, founder of Amazon—the company, not the river basin—once instructed his team, "If we want . . . Amazon to be a place where builders can build, we need . . . to eliminate communication, not encourage it. When you view effective communication across groups as a 'defect,' the solutions to your problems start to look quite different from traditional ones."[5]) Contrast this to innovation inside of most organizations, where innovation is centralized, experiments are expensive whether they fail or succeed, and over-communication leads to consensus that kills disruptive ideas. Communication invites vetocracy; in large organizations it is common for an idea to be killed by a single naysayer. Unanimity feels safer.

3. Knowledge compounds

The search for novelty, the hunt for surprises, is what makes the ecosystem extraordinarily resilient, vibrant, and alive. Innovations like eyes or lungs or touch or smell might be considered improvements that help creatures survive and thrive. But they can also be viewed as inevitable results of a search with no final objective that is accumulating information about the world. If you keep trying new designs through mutation, even though there's no defined objective, eventually you will discover that light exists and can be useful. Seeking surprises and gathering information—or in other words, gaining access to an ever-widening array of building blocks—is what enables new discoveries. The best innovations are those that enable and power further innovations. Resilient organizations are effective at accumulating knowledge and discovering assets, needs, and solutions outside the corporation that might prove useful.

What's the lesson for small and large organizations? To manufacture serendipity, you need to seek surprise (or novelty), to collect as much knowledge and as many building blocks as you can to rearrange into new combinations.[6] Cheap and fast experimentation, at the margins, will increase the likelihood of you encountering insights. Your process will be limited by constraints to help you manage finite resources, not by lofty objectives. In other words, seek novelty for novelty's sake, without a clear plan for what will happen next, and you will learn what is possible.

The best innovators are treasure hunters, looking for the next chest full of jewels around the corner, without a clear plan in mind. In retrospect, the search makes sense when the discovery is made, but in the moment, the collection of knowledge can seem random and unfocused.

As an example of how this works, think about how your career has developed. You are likely not currently doing the thing you thought you would be doing years ago, but because of serendipity, the actual path may be better than you could have designed. When you look back, you see building blocks of knowledge, sometimes gathered from unexpected sources, that enable you to excel at what you're doing now. Steve Jobs famously audited a calligraphy class in college and used that knowledge to apply creative fonts in his Apple computers, making the experience suredly better for users. If Jobs's goal was to become the CEO of the most transformative consumer computer company in the world, taking a calligraphy class would not have been on the checklist of ways to prepare.

But he took the class because it was interesting, and it later proved to be very useful.

Examples abound of corporations that developed new business models by savoring surprises. Amazon famously stumbled into its profitable AWS business through experimentation around its own needs for data storage and management. Google developed its popular Gmail service initially as an internal tool to enable better search of archived emails. Nvidia's valuation rocketed after it leaned into customers' use of the company's graphics chips in parallel to achieve massive breakthroughs in speed for nongraphic applications.

Experiment at the margins within constraints, in pursuit of what is interesting, and good things are more likely to happen. This is what creates resilience and outsized outcomes. In an increasingly decentralized world, this means that for corporations, experimentation and "treasure seeking" will only become harder to do internally and easier to do outside the traditional boundaries of the corporation, with small, empowered teams (i.e., startups). In the world of business, startups are a "cheap" form of experimentation, the equivalent of the Amazon's individual organisms where mutation happens.

Understanding an organization's barriers to experimentation, especially the incentives at play, is necessary for developing organizational willingness to try new things, even things that might fail. Incentives matter a lot. Surprisingly, there are many parallels between a large corporation's inability to take on risk and the modern mismanagement of forest land and wildfires in the western United States. Large and devastating wildfires have become an annual occurrence in western states, where people now talk about a regular "fire season." It doesn't have to be that way, but systemic optimization for near-term incentives has created a situation that seems simultaneously easy and impossible to fix. Everyone knows what needs to be done, but no one is able to do it.

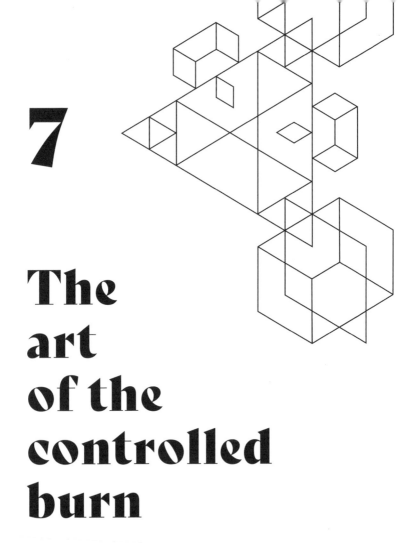

7

The art of the controlled burn

Align incentives with objectives.

By looking at the growth rings of trees, scientists can see when droughts occurred or when rain was plentiful. They can see when trees were under some kind of stress, like fire. In the San Juan National Forest in the US state of Colorado, scientists study fire scars in tree rings to count the frequency and intensity of forest fires. Using this method, they can track fire trends as far back as 1686 and measure how often at least one tree in a site was scarred by fire and how often at least 25 percent of the trees in a site encountered flames. The remarkable thing about the research is that it has shown that around the year 1880, intense fires almost completely stopped in the San Juan National Forest.

A similar thing happened in my home state of California. Prior to the 1849 gold rush, scientists estimate that 4.5 million acres of forest burned every year in the state. Lightning fires burned for months, and native tribes frequently cleared the land of dead vegetation with fire. For much of the subsequent century, as the state's population grew and built homes, towns, and parks in rural areas, firefighters worked fervently to extinguish flames to save property and lives. The efforts were quite successful, and by the 1950s and 1960s, only 250,000 acres burned each year, on average, in California.

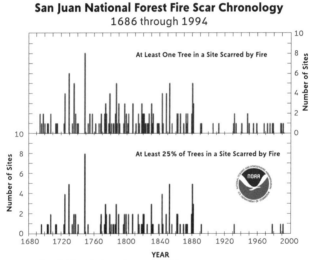

San Juan National Forest Fire Scar Chronology
1686 through 1994

Source: National Climatic Data Center, NOAA

The near eradication of wildfire was a remarkable achievement of human ingenuity over the natural environment, the result of a determined effort by the residents, governments, and firefighters of western states to reduce the variability and volatility of fires.

Unfortunately, as a direct result of the fire eradication effort, forests in California are now *ten times* denser than they would be naturally. Unlike the Amazon, the forests in California are not resilient, and the difference is the degree of human intervention, of top-down hierarchical management.

When dry weather and other conditions are right, fires now burn much hotter and faster than they once did. In 2018, a devastating wildfire known as the Camp Fire destroyed the town of Paradise, California, where my great-great-grandparents once lived and are buried. Although it was particularly destructive in terms of loss of life and property, the Camp Fire's duration and coverage were not unique compared with other recent fires. Over the last several years, a wave of massive, uncontrolled fires has swept across the western United States. In August and September of 2020 alone, five of the six largest fires in the recorded history of California up to that time raged, and the "fire season" stretched well beyond its typical duration.

This unfortunate trend is likely to continue, and in many ways it is the direct result of dramatic institutional effectiveness directed toward what is now, in retrospect, understood to be the wrong objective—fire eradication instead of fire management. We prioritized efficiency and the illusion of near-term safety over long-term resilience, and we are now paying the price. The system of incentives created safety in the near term, but danger in the long term.

The irony is that there is widespread agreement among experts about what to do to solve the problem of uncontrollable fires. The best approach is a persistent strategy of controlled burns to limit the dry vegetation that fuels the spread and intensity of fires. In a controlled burn, a land manager purposely sets alight a defined area of land. When repeated, an effective strategy of controlled burns creates a checkerboard map of burned and unburned areas, limiting the fuel and path a wildfire can travel.

In California between 1999 and 2017, land managers burned, on average, thirteen thousand acres per year.[1] They might as well have burned nothing. By 2018, experts believed the state had accumulated a "fire debt" of about twenty million acres.[2] To put that into perspective, it means an area the size of Maine might need to burn before California can restabilize.

State leaders have recently passed laws and signed memoranda of understanding to undertake more controlled burning, but little real progress has been made. Everyone knows what to do, but no one seems able to act because of sticky incentives and ineffective governance.

If you are a land manager and you start a controlled burn, there is a risk you may lose control of the fire. This form of failure can be extremely expensive, and many people are incentivized to not allow it. Failure is too costly to the land manager, and there is no individual upside to compensate for the risk.

Similarly, the benefits of a controlled burn will only accrue over the long term, if at all. The number of years between significant fires is likely greater than any land manager's tenure. If a fire comes, the chances are good it will come on someone else's watch.

Compounding the difficulty, rules make controlled burns hard to execute. In California, purposeful burns have to comply with the Clean Air Act, which limits emissions from human-caused events. Of course, air quality impacts from prescribed burns are *tiny* compared with the damage months of widespread fires can do to the air. (Images of San Francisco in 2020 bathed in an eerie orange glow from smoke are a testament to this.)

Rules, incentives, and governance—too many people who can say "no"—make it difficult for individuals to act within the confines of the existing system, and so nothing gets done.

Forests continue to become denser, and large fires rage out of control, with greater intensity and frequency.

For the last one hundred years, land managers and firefighters have become very effective at putting small fires out immediately when they happen. The systems are optimized for it. Governments have invested in the equipment and regulations to enable it. What they have not optimized for, because of sticky incentives, is the art of the controlled burn.

Similarly, many of our large institutions, including our scaled corporations, are like the dense forests in California. Decades of avoidance of "small fires," as evidenced by a relentless focus on capital efficiency, renders institutions extremely fragile in the face of inevitable shocks. When the "fire" comes, it burns quickly and with intensity. And although we cannot predict the timing, we know that fire will inevitably come. As long as RONA, ROIC, and IRR remain the primary metrics by which we measure corporate success, we should expect corporate failures to become increasingly swift and painful, with widespread impact—the financial equivalent of the Camp Fire.

Executives are incentivized to act like the land managers in California. Innovation theater is the corporate equivalent of burning thirteen thousand acres yearly in the face of a twenty-million-acre fire debt. Most large companies have piled up extraordinary "innovation debt."

The solution for corporations is the same for land managers seeking to prevent uncontrollable fires: adopt a strategy of "controlled burns," a willingness to tolerate some inefficiency and bounded risk in the near term in exchange for long-term resilience. If innovation is the result of learning, of systematic conversion of assumptions into knowledge, then it must be, by definition, capital inefficient in the near term. In a corporation, a strategy of "controlled burns" looks like a strategy of rapid experimentation, focused on learning and building future optionality.

Of course, for corporate managers, like land managers, the incentives are challenging:

- There is too much at stake for an individual manager if an experiment fails.
- The benefits of experimentation may not be realized by the current executive.
- Existing rules hinder experimentation, whether by a corporation, market, or government.
- Governance systems provide opportunities for too many people to say "no" and stop experimentation before it yields results.

Contrast this with the incentives that drive entrepreneurs to "play with fire":

- There is too much to lose if the entrepreneur's startup experiment fails, so he or she will do just about anything to make it work quickly.
- The benefits of the experimentation must be realized during the entrepreneur's tenure, and it is within his or her control to determine that.
- The startup allows the entrepreneur to work outside existing rules and norms and sometimes even regulations that apply only to incumbents.
- Entrepreneurs operate with limited governance designed to encourage experimentation, learning, and pivots, prioritizing disruption over preservation of the status quo.

Entrepreneurs work within a system that enables them to master the art of controlled burns. The solution for corporate executives is not to so radically change the corporate structure that it upends incentives that drive them to eradicate variability but rather to leverage the risk takers outside of the organization who are incentivized to play with fire. To state it again, corporations must learn how to push experimentation out to the edges (and beyond) of the corporation; the good news is that there is a willing group of people—entrepreneurs—operating within a system of incentives who are poised to do the things corporations cannot. This is why the innovation success of most large corporations over the next few decades will be determined by the quality of their engagement with startups. Deliberate fires, like startups, can be thought of as a *purposeful* form of experimentation at the margins.

The Amazon rainforest builds resilience through random mutations at the level of individual cells or organisms. It is impractical to think that scaled organizations will ever enable that kind of full-throttled, chaotic, and natural experimentation. Perhaps a middle ground exists for large corporations, where controlled experimentation is allowed within clear constraints. It's possible that "purposeful burns" might become more acceptable in the business world. New ventures, particularly in the form of independent, external startups, are a corporation's best access to experimentation that works like cellular mutation or controlled burns. These ventures allow big corporations to experiment in a way that limits downside risk in the initial investment without limiting upside opportunity. This is especially useful in a world that is becoming more decentralized.

8

Manufacturing serendipity

Seek novelty to create strategic optionality.

In 2020, a thirty-one-year-old man named Hafthor "Thor" Bjornsson deadlifted 501 kilograms, or more than 1,100 pounds, and set a new world record. He lifted one kilogram more than the previous record, held by a Brit with whom he had had a longstanding feud; after the lift Thor said he felt he could have lifted more, but was only focused on breaking the old record, almost out of spite.

Thor was born in Iceland, with certain qualities that gave him an edge when breaking the world record for the heaviest deadlift. He's 6'9" tall, for one thing. But he had to train extensively to pull off his record lift. In addition to regular, strenuous workouts, Thor had to consume up to ten thousand calories a day, with a high-protein diet, to build muscle. It takes work to eat ten thousand calories a day! Thor had to eat six meals daily to squeeze in those calories. At the time of his record lift, Thor weighed about 450 pounds. The strain of the lift caused Thor to bleed from his eye sockets.

Doing something like this is not easy. No one had ever done this before! And it is hard to imagine anyone will do it again anytime soon (although it is likely someone will eventually!). Thor chose hardship, strain, and difficulty to build the muscle required to break the world record.

Despite his enormous natural size, Thor could not have performed his record lift without putting his body through tremendous strain for years before. To produce muscle growth, Thor had to progressively apply loads of stress greater than what his body had previously adapted to. The tension in the muscle created better muscle control. It also caused muscle damage and metabolic stress that led to repairs and increases in muscle growth and strength over time.

It is a slow and painful process, but a necessary one for breaking world records in lifting. Growth requires tension and stress. There is no other way in weightlifting, in life, or in business.

Here's the irony: When people build companies, they naturally try to minimize stress and tension while still achieving growth. As companies grow, they optimize their systems of governance, incentives, talent recruitment and retention, and the processes by which they operate to eradicate risk, increase predictability, and conserve what has already been built. They apply top-down, hierarchical, and objective-driven approaches to increase efficiency and remove variability. Capital efficiency becomes the primary goal, and as I have tried to explain at great length in this book, the problem is that innovation is not capital efficient.

Yet people try. They seek growth, they seek insights, they seek innovation without having to experience the pain and tension that comes from stressing a business model to do something new. If Thor applied the same strategy of limited stress and tension, he would never have built the strength or achieved the growth required to break the world record.

When it comes to innovation, variability is your friend. You can't get the gains without putting the system under tension and stress. You have to be willing to risk failure.

Experimentation requires failure

Gary Klein, who studies the science of insights, explained the dilemma well in his book *Seeing What Others Don't*. According to Klein, in our organizations we try to simultaneously reduce errors while increasing insights, and the reality is that you can't have both an error-free operation *and* learning and insights. There must be an acceptable amount of error, of inefficiency, allowed to generate insights.[1]

Entrepreneurs know this well. There is a tremendous amount of inefficiency in startups but also an incredibly rapid pace of learning. Startups are actually *optimized* for both inefficiency and learning.

If you want transformative, empowering innovation, you need to be willing to experience stress, tension, and inefficiency in your organization. There is no other way. You have to find a way to create tension that helps you source weak signals. Scaled organizations are designed to toss aside weak beliefs—those things that contradict what we already believe to be true. But we often learn by *centering* on weak beliefs, taking them seriously instead of explaining them away or trying to throw them out.

Anomalies wanted

Clayton Christensen loved woodworking. He hung a wooden sign that he made outside his office at Harvard Business School that read: *Anomalies Wanted.* Christensen loved to find (and actively sought out) anomalies because he recognized that finding the unexpected can lead to the greatest advances in knowledge. Anomalies drive us to test and improve and change our theories about how the world works. Anomalies are a form of tension that makes us stronger, like Thor's workouts before his big lift.

Most organizations don't do this very well. Leaders want to identify the next big thing, so they undertake an exercise in analyzing trends, for example. But trends are misleading. By the time a trend is established, many of the opportunities it presents have most likely already been exploited. Companies need to understand trends, of course, but an understanding of trends is very unlikely to challenge status quo thinking or lead to any meaningful insight.

You have to be willing to break your business model to grow it substantially. You have to actively find ways to challenge your current beliefs or the assumptions of your organization. Most of those assumptions come in some form of "what worked before will work again." As the pace of change increases, that set of assumptions will become increasingly less reliable, even misleading.

It is in doing the hard things—putting in the reps and being willing to question the status quo—that we learn and grow. If you put in the hard work, you will uncover anomalies, and anomalies are the building blocks of insights.

You need insights—a lot of them—if you want to compete in the weird future that is coming. The problem is that it is hard to predict ahead of time which activities will lead to transformative insights. We can learn a lot about insights from the world of venture investing.

Early-stage venture capital is what is called a "power law asset class," meaning the majority of returns are driven by a few outliers. Venture capitalists know they can make a lot of bets that fail, and that's the point. They know that when breakthroughs occur, those few winning investments will more than make up for all the failures. Successful venture capitalists also know that making decisions based on what has worked in the past—pattern matching—reduces the variety in the portfolio and makes it less likely that the portfolio will contain outliers that drive performance. The goal when dealing with a power law asset class, like insights or early-stage ventures, is to create a portfolio with a lot of variety.

In a normal distribution, like public equities, a smaller pool of investments will earn you an average return. In early-stage venture investing, a portfolio of only twenty to thirty investments is unlikely to produce industry-average returns consistently.

The Power Law Curve

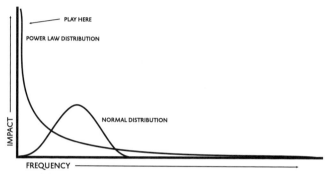

Source: High Alpha Innovation

In venture investing, the average rate of unicorn production is only 1–2 percent,[2] which varies across geographies and sectors. Therefore, to be a successful venture investor, one might argue that you must choose to diversify your investments across a broad number of companies and sectors because there is no clear indication ahead of time which investments will turn out to be outliers.

If you believe the asset class you focus on follows power law distribution, you will want to have the most diversified portfolio possible. Here is the amazing thing about power law distributions: if your portfolio is diversified enough, individual losses don't matter, because the outsized successes will make up the difference for those losses.

Insights are like venture investments. Most insights are inconsequential, but a few end up pushing you in entirely different directions and can lead to outsized success. To access those unicorn insights, you need a portfolio that is diversified. You need to try a lot of things. You need a lot of reps. And you need to stop pattern matching because pattern matching kills variance. That means you must stop choosing experiments based on their ability to reinforce what you already know. It means you must stop choosing experiments by committee. It means you need to run far more experiments and do more weird things. You need to understand that insights are a power law asset class, and your goal is to capture maximum variance.

Like many engineering teams, the group responsible for managing Microsoft's search engine, Bing, regularly performs A/B tests to measure the effectiveness of changes to the product's design. Large, statistically relevant A/B tests are a common approach for screening the viability and attractiveness of minor changes in software code. In an A/B test, a team deploys two alternative versions of a product change in a limited release before selecting which change to make permanent. The optimal strategy for running A/B tests depends on whether the majority of improvements come from typical innovations or from rare and unpredictable successes. If insights come rarely, it is better to perform more experiments. Researchers who studied the efforts of the Bing team at Microsoft discovered that 2 percent of the ideas were responsible for 75 percent of gains.[3] Their conclusion? When there are no outlier results, it is best to "perform thorough prior screening of potential innovations, and to run a few high-powered precise experiments." However, when a small percentage of experiments drive most of the gains, it is "advantageous to run many small experiments, and to test a large number of ideas in hopes of finding a big winner."

In his widely read book, *Atomic Habits*, the author James Clear tells the story of a photography teacher who divided his class into two groups. The first group was dubbed the quantity group, and their mission was to create as many photos as they could over the course of the semester. Their grade would depend entirely on the number of photos they took. The second group was called the quality group, and their objective was to create a single, perfect image during the semester. The quality of that one photo would determine their grade for the semester. To get an A, the photo had to be nearly perfect.

You likely know what happened. At the end of the term, the teacher was surprised to learn that the quantity group produced all of the best photos. The quantity group spent the semester experimenting with lighting and composition, taking as many photos as they could, and learning from their mistakes. The quality group thought a lot about perfection, but they had little to show for their efforts in the end.

Putting in the reps

Pablo Picasso lived to be ninety-one years old and was extraordinarily prolific over his lifetime. According to James Clear, "Researchers have catalogued 26,075 pieces of art created by Picasso and some people believe the total number is closer to 50,000. . . . Picasso lived for a total of 33,403 days. With 26,075 published works, that means Picasso averaged 1 new piece of artwork every day of his life from age 20 until his death at age 91. He created something new, every day, for 71 years."[4] Similarly, Bach composed twenty pages of music per day.[5] Thomas Edison published a new patent every ten to twelve days of his adult life.[6] The greatest artists are usually, not coincidentally, also the most prolific artists.

You must put in the reps to learn and accumulate knowledge. Novelty and knowledge compound over time. In business, this can be done in a structured and systematic way through rapid and inexpensive experimentation. *In the face of an unknown future, the best way to maximize returns and minimize risk is to run as many experiments as you can at the lowest possible cost per experiment.* It is very hard to predict which experiments are going to create the most impactful insights, so you need to run a lot of experiments.

Your job as an innovator is to seek anomalies. Experiments uncover anomalies. Anomalies are building blocks to insight. And insight is what creates serendipity.

Disneylandia

I grew up in Southern California, close enough to Disneyland that on summer nights at 9 p.m. we could see the fireworks from my sisters' bedroom on the second floor of our house. So, Disneyland was very much part of the local lore growing up. We went often. Friends worked there. Some were caught jumping the fence at Disneyland and were put in "Disneyland jail." It was a local teenage hangout of sorts. The story of how Disneyland came to be is fascinating because it is an example of how the search for what is interesting, novel, and surprising for its own sake can lead to path-altering discoveries.

By the 1940s, Walt Disney had achieved wild success in the field of animation. He had created an entirely new industry from scratch, revolutionizing how the public thought about animation and feature films. But he had also lived through many low points as an entrepreneur. His businesses had come close to the brink of complete ruin more than once.

During World War II, Disney's animators played an active role in producing films to help the war cause. After the war ended, Disney was eager to shift his attention back to commercial feature films. But it was hard and slow going. There was more competition, and the costs of producing films at the level of quality Disney demanded had skyrocketed. At every turn, things seemed to be more difficult and less rewarding than they had once been. Employees complained that Disney seemed frustrated and was taking it out on them.

He began disengaging from the business and hired a management team to run the day-to-day, although they were frustrated about the lack of clarity in their roles and responsibilities. Disney was anxious and aimless, without advancing projects to engage him wholeheartedly.

An assistant suggested that Disney take a trip to get away and go to a railroad fair in Chicago, even though he had just returned from a trip to Hawaii. She told him he still needed to relax. Disney had a friend who was a railroad enthusiast and who always seemed relaxed, so the two of them took the Super Chief from Pasadena to Chicago for the fair. At one point along the way, the president of the Santa Fe Railroad invited Disney and his friend to ride in the engine and pull the cord to blow the whistle. Disney's friend said that Disney pulled the cord long and hard, and when he returned to his seat, "just sat there, staring into space, smiling and smiling."[7] Disney's friend said he had never seen him look so happy.

When Disney was growing up in Marceline, Missouri, his uncle Mike, a railroad engineer, would bring candy to the Disney farm. Young Walt rode on the trains selling candy and soda. He associated fond memories with trains and thought of them as recreation and a way to decompress from the pressures of business.

Disney returned from the trip to Chicago absolutely obsessed with trains. He bought model trains for his nephews for Christmas in 1947 and treated himself to something he said he had wanted his entire life: an electric train. This was no ordinary train. With the help of a machinist in the studio shop, Disney built an elaborate layout in the office. It was large enough to fill a two-car garage with miniature towns, tunnels, and moveable bridges. Disney was hooked.

From there, he considered acquiring a train big enough to ride on. The pursuit became all-consuming. The train became his job. Before long, Disney decided to make the train himself with help from some studio employees. Fabricating the train became his passion, and he spent Saturdays at the studio in his work clothes, sometimes with kids in tow, working on the project.

He told a colleague at the time, "You know, it does me some good to come down here and find out I don't know everything."[8] Things were fun again.

Just before Christmas in 1948, Disney laid out three hundred feet of track on the soundstage and fired up the engine of his new locomotive. He was ecstatic.

But others around him were frustrated and confused. A film critic from the *New York Times* said, after meeting with Disney, that she came away "feeling sad" because Disney, the man with such an impact on film and entertainment and such a productive imagination, was now spending most of his time playing with trains.[9]

The Disneys purchased a new home perfect for laying out a track in the backyard, as employees at the studio wondered about Disney's commitment to the business. He remained involved in projects like *Cinderella*, but employees complained that he was no longer an artist and was much more business-like than he had once been.

The trains became the start of a much larger and more ambitious project that began taking shape in Disney's mind. Around the same time Disney fell in love with trains, he began playing with and building miniatures—furniture, figurines, and entire scenes of small-town life. These were supposed to be for the train but became an additional pastime to take his mind off the studio when things became too complicated. He began scouring catalogs and newspapers for sales of miniatures and attending miniature shows. He came up with an idea to build an entire miniature American turn-of-the-century village and then display it in cases across the country.

He eventually called his exhibition Disneylandia.

A columnist at the time who visited the show marveled at Disney's work and asked, "Why does he do it?" To which Disney answered effectively, "I have no idea."[10]

But Disney knew what he was doing. In his pursuit of novelty and interestingness, he slowly stumbled into his biggest idea. It is hard to know precisely when the idea took shape, but Disney had decided to build an amusement park.

We know how the story played out after that. The path to Disneyland's eventual success was filled with twists and turns, and required unusual determination.

When Disney began playing with trains, everyone thought he had lost his mind, but Disney pursued what he thought was interesting, and he took the building blocks he had accumulated in storytelling, entertainment, miniatures, and rides and created in Disneyland a new industry, just as he had done with animation.

Novelty and surprise are worthy pursuits. They are both a means to an end and a desirable destination in and of themselves.

Disney's story is unique because of its scale and impact, but it's not uncommon in the roundabout way that the idea of Disneyland came together.

It is hard to think of a precursor to any vital invention that was created with that ultimate invention in mind. The building blocks used to create an invention rarely resemble the final product.

Interestingness

Perhaps the best example of this principle in practice is described by AI researchers Kenneth Stanley and Joel Lehman in their remarkable book, *Why Greatness Cannot Be Planned: The Myth of the Objective*. The authors explain how they developed a computer program for generating images that produced extraordinary results with profound implications for how we all pursue lofty objectives.

In 2006, Stanley and colleagues launched an online program called Picbreeder, which allowed users to "breed pictures." The program started by generating ten to twenty random images—mere blobs—and then instructed the user to select any image. From the selection, the program would generate ten to twenty "children," variations on the chosen image. At each round, users were instructed to select the image they found most "interesting." According to Stanley and Lehman, "the hope was that by allowing visitors to breed the pictures they find most interesting, over time they would end up breeding works of art that please them, even if the visitors were not artists."[11]

Initially, the researchers found that users lost interest in the exercise after twenty or so generations of images. So, they tweaked the program to allow for the sharing of images so that users could continue to evolve an image someone else had already produced. They knew that evolution works best over many generations, and twenty generations wasn't enough to produce compelling images.

Once users were allowed to share images online, they could hand off their results to someone else who could continue "breeding" pictures and taking the images far beyond twenty generations. The researchers could never have predicted the results: after many generations, the initial blobs mutated into recognizable images of objects like cars, skulls, dolphins, cameras, and mugs. The focus on "interestingness," without a clear end objective in mind, led to "discoveries."

Now here's the counterintuitive lesson they also learned: One might assume that by beginning with an end objective or image in mind—a goal to produce an image that looks like, for example, the Statue of Liberty—one would eventually reach the objective. At each round one might select the image that most closely resembles the Statue of Liberty, and after many generations the images would evolve into the end goal. Intuition would tell us that such a path might be more efficient, in fact, than haphazardly selecting "interesting" images until something better and more realistic appears, but without a clear end goal in mind. In fact, the opposite is true. Once you find an image on Picbreeder, it's often impossible to evolve the same image again from scratch, even though it was clearly within the set of discoverable possibilities.

The researchers confirmed the paradox by instructing a computer program to run through thousands of generations of image evolution to arrive at predetermined target images.

They began by choosing a target image from those users who had already discovered and published on the site. Then, at every generation, they instructed the computer to select the image most closely resembling the target image. The result, every time, was complete failure, even after thousands of generations.

The lesson? According to Stanley and Lehman, "Objectives are well and good when they are sufficiently modest, but things get a lot more complicated when they're more ambitious. In fact, objectives actually become *obstacles* towards more exciting achievements, like those involving discovery, creativity, invention, or innovation—or even achieving true happiness. In other words . . . the greatest achievements become *less likely* when they are made objectives."[12] Therefore, the key to achieving lofty objectives is to seek interestingness and novelty, collect the novelty because it compounds, and let oneself be surprised by what happens in the end.

Stanley and Lehman explain that "unpredictability is the rule rather than the exception in almost any situation with an ambitious objective":

> The first engine was not invented with airplanes in mind, but of course the Wright brothers needed an engine to build a flying machine. Microwave technology

was not first invented for ovens, but rather was part of magnetron power tubes that drove radars. . . . Stories of delayed revelations and serendipitous discovery expose the danger of objectives: If your objective was to invent a microwave oven, you would not be working on radars. If you wanted to build a flying machine (as countless failed inventors did over the years), you wouldn't spend the next few decades instead trying to invent an engine. If you were like Charles Babbage in the 1820s and wanted to build a computer, you wouldn't dedicate the rest of your life to refining vacuum tube technology. But in all these cases, what you would never do is exactly what you should have done. The paradox is that the key stepping stones were perfected only by people *without* the ultimate objective of building microwaves, airplanes, or computers. The structure of the search space—the great room of all possible things—is just plain weird. It's so bad that the objective can actually *distract* you from its own stepping stones! If you think too much about computers you'll never think of vacuum tubes. The problem is that ambitious objectives are often *deceptive*. They dangle a false promise of achievement if we pursue them purposefully. But strangely in the end we often must give them up to ever have the chance of reaching them.[13]

Said differently, the secret to manufacturing serendipity is to seek out and cherish novelty and to accumulate the information one learns along the way. The primary job of the innovator is to convert assumptions into knowledge by gathering insights. The best innovators do this systematically, through rapid and cheap experiments that poke holes in status quo beliefs. They are searching for secrets and understanding them before the rest of the world does.

Secrets

Andrew Carnegie's discovery of such a secret is what led him to become one of the richest men in history. Carnegie is famous for two things: making a fortune in the steel industry (sometimes with ruthless means), and then giving much of his fortune away in constructing libraries across the United States.

The key to his initial success in steel? Carnegie was one of the first to apply chemistry to the production of steel effectively. When Carnegie first began his career in the industry, he said, "Chemistry in the United States was an almost unknown agent in connection with the manufacture of pig iron" (a key ingredient in steel production). At the time, according to Carnegie:

> The blast-furnace manager of that day was usually a rude bully . . . who in addition to his other acquirements was able to knock down a man now and then as a lesson to the other unruly spirits under him. He was supposed to diagnose the condition of the furnace by instinct, to possess some almost supernatural power of divination, like his congener in the country districts who was reputed to be able to locate an oil well or water supply by means of a hazel rod. He was a veritable quack doctor who applied whatever remedies occurred to him for the troubles of his patient.[14]

In the 1870s, when Carnegie was starting out, ores and other inputs to the steel production process were inconsistent in quality and composition. According to Carnegie, "The Lucy Furnace was out of one trouble and into another, owing to the great variety of ores, limestone, and coke which were then supplied with little or no regard to their component parts. This state of affairs became intolerable to us."[15]

Carnegie decided, against conventional wisdom, to turn to chemistry:

> We finally decided to dispense with the rule-of-thumb-and-intuition manager, and to place [Henry M. Curry] in charge of the furnace. . . . The next step taken was to find a chemist as Mr. Curry's assistant and guide. We

found the man in a learned German, Dr. Fricke, and great secrets did the doctor open up to us. Iron stone from mines that had a high reputation was now found to contain ten, fifteen, and even twenty per cent less iron than it had been credited with. Mines that hitherto had a poor reputation we found to be now yielding superior ore. The good was bad and the bad was good, and everything was topsy-turvy. Nine tenths of all the uncertainties of pig-iron making were dispelled under the burning sun of chemical knowledge.[16]

Carnegie and his team discovered that they could work with low-quality materials; the right mix of materials mattered most, no matter the purity of the inputs. This new knowledge led Carnegie to proclaim the following:

What fools we had been! But then there was this consolation: we were not as great fools as our competitors. It was years after we had taken chemistry to guide us that it was said by the proprietors of some other furnaces that they could not afford to employ a chemist. Had they known the truth then, they would have known that they could not afford to be without one. Looking back it seems pardonable to record that we were the first to employ a chemist at blast furnaces—something our competitors pronounced extravagant.[17]

Through the scientific application of chemistry, Carnegie was able to arbitrage his supplies, buying inputs from mines his competitors believed to be inferior. For years, Carnegie's competitors continued to throw away inputs, believing them to be worthless when, unbeknownst to them, chemistry had proven them to be of great purity and value.

The manufacture of serendipity begins with experimentation. Experiments reveal anomalies. Accumulation of anomalies compounds to create knowledge, and knowledge generates insights. Serendipity can be manufactured through consistent access to insights.

If you want more serendipity, you should probably be running more experiments that challenge your existing assumptions and beliefs.

Moving away from where you've been

Pursuing anomalies, or novelty, should not be considered aimless or uncertain. Novelty is achieved simply by moving away from where you've been already. In contrast, choosing a long-term goal and charting a path toward that distant destination is hard. Deviating from the past is much simpler! Seeking out novelty is the fastest way to accumulate data about the future. So, take action to create data, and pursue novelty.

This is not new advice. Others have explained this in the past as the need to create collisions. Bell Labs was famously housed in a building with long corridors that created collisions between specialists from different fields. Many people know about this, but in practice it is hard to do. It's more than coming to conferences; it's more than reading widely. It likely requires dramatically increasing the quantity and rigor of experimentation that you are pursuing.

You likely need to run far more structured experiments that challenge the status quo. And you need to find ways to reduce the cost of your experiments. Often this means running experiments at the margins, at the level of the individual cell or organism in your organization, with limited communication. For most large organizations, the best way to experiment quickly, cheaply, and at the margins is to build external ventures with a high degree of separation from core operations. The more different from the core, the more separation is required for the venture to succeed.

You need variance in your insight portfolio if you want unicorn breakthroughs. That means increased sample sizes. Avoid pattern matching. Avoid making decisions by committee about which experiments to pursue or what to do with the results of experiments.

You can increase your variance by focusing on horizontal, not vertical, learning. Vertical learning is when you go deeper into things you already know, searching for data to confirm beliefs you already have. Horizontal learning is when you go outside your organization's sphere of knowledge to learn things that may challenge status quo beliefs. If you work at a bank, you should be open to running experiments far beyond the world of fintech. If you work at a pharma company, you should be open to running experiments far beyond the world of molecules. If you want insights, you must move away from what you already know and understand.

Finally, you are likely acting in an environment of limited constraints. For most readers of this book, it would not be a good idea to tell your CFO that you have seen the light and need permission to go play with trains and miniatures to "see what happens." Walt Disney was in a unique position with a well-merited reputation that led others to give him freedom to operate. You are likely in a position where it would be impossible to throw out goals and objectives altogether, even though doing so *would be more likely to lead to successful outcomes.* You would likely have a hard time convincing your peers that this is true, and even if you were successful, time would likely run out before you could demonstrate adequate success.

If you can only get away with implementing one recommendation from this chapter, do this: instead of judging possible experiments for their potential to "succeed," choose experiments based on their ability to spawn more experiments, enabling you to accumulate more knowledge over time. Novelty and learning compound. Which experiments will most likely produce the most surprises and more questions? Do those. Which experiments are more likely to uncover anomalies? Which experiments are more likely to produce a result the organization wants to reject? Those experiments will help you center on weak beliefs and generate the nonconsensus insights that will help your organization become more resilient.

9

Selecting shots

Random experimentation is unwise; the best experiments lead to more experiments.

The NBA's adoption of the three-point line in the 1978–1979 season was the most consequential rule change in modern sports. It forever altered the game.

At the time, many wondered if the rule change was a gimmick that wouldn't last. The three-point rule had been a staple of the defunct American Basketball Association, and some NBA coaches who had come over from the old league championed the change. Still, such a dramatic alteration to an established game was hard for many to accept.

Seattle player Fred Brown predicted that "a lot of teams are going to lose more games than they are going to win because of [the three-point rule]." Unable to imagine the devastating shot accuracy of a future Steph Curry, Brown suggested that "there will be some guys who think they can make it every time, so they'll be launching them all night."[1] (Ironically, Fred

Brown ended up leading the league in three-pointers the first season the rule was adopted.[2])

Regarding the rule change, Bullet coach Dick Motta said at the time, "It'll prove to be interesting, but I don't think the league will attract 10,000 more fans a week because of it."[3]

It has indeed proven to be interesting and has shown that prediction is hard.

Since the rule change, the game has changed dramatically and attracted millions of new fans. The increase in the fan base can't be attributed entirely to the three-point rule, of course, but it is clear the change has led to more exciting—and high-scoring—games. The last time an NBA team won without scoring a single three-point shot was in 2016.[4] In that game, the Miami Heat beat the Charlotte Hornets on the road while going 0-for-9 in three-point attempts. It's hard to imagine a professional basketball team doing that ever again.

The three-point rate (the percentage of all shot attempts that come from beyond the three-point line) increased slowly at first after the rule change, as teams learned strategies for adjusting to the change. But between 2011 and 2021, the use of three-point shots increased markedly, from 22.2 percent in 2010–2011 to 39.2 percent in the 2020–2021 season.[5]

Teams have learned that mid-range shots don't pay. Average points per shot are highest for shots taken near the rim or beyond the three-point line. Three-point shots go in 36 percent of the time, and ten-foot shots go in 40 percent of the time.[6] But those ten-foot shots, when they are successful, are only worth two points. One shot is worth 50 percent more than another shot taken, with a similar chance of success, only inches away. In a game where efficiency matters and billions of dollars are at stake, teams have found a path to success: teams that make more three-point shots are more likely to win.

According to one fan's analysis, although three-pointers are slightly more difficult than mid-range jumpers (meaning they have a lower chance of going in the basket), they are more efficient: "The average 3-pointer is .16 points per shot (PPS) more efficient than the average midrange jumper. Most NBA teams have a pace at around 100 possessions per 48 minutes. So, over the course of a game, we would expect a team that shoots only [3-pointers] to outscore a team that only shoots midrange jumpers by 16 points!"[7]

Half of NBA teams are taking more than 40 percent of their shots from beyond the three-point line now, and there is no sign the trend is diminishing. According to the Dallas

Mavericks's director of quantitative research and development, "I don't think we've reached the upper limit yet . . . I think when you start getting into around 60 to 65 percent 3-point rate, that's probably where you're getting toward more diminishing returns."[8]

What matters more, the quality or quantity of shots taken? The answer to the age-old question is, "both." Teams that win take more shots, but they also take them more strategically.

The implications for an organization that wants to innovate are obvious: create and take more *high-quality* shots on goal. As we have discussed at length in this book, in the face of an unknown future, the best way to maximize returns and minimize risk is to run as many experiments as possible at the lowest possible cost per experiment. The solution to organizational sclerosis is more experimentation: faster, cheaper, and weirder. About experiments, we have also learned the following:

- Innovators are professional insight gatherers; their primary job is to convert assumptions to knowledge on behalf of the organization.

- Insights are a power law asset class; insight gatherers should seek variance in their insight portfolio (as many insights as possible across a broad range of topics).

- Experimentation is best done at the margins, at the

equivalent of the organizational cell or organism, where failure is cheap but success can catch on.

- Decentralization empowers small teams and individuals to access expertise, capital, and ideas.
- Pursuit of novelty without objective (but within constraints) is surprisingly the most efficient way to achieve outsized outcomes.
- Experiments should be designed to surface anomalies, to challenge—not reinforce—the status quo.
- The systems used by a scaled organization to run efficiently and safely—its governance, talent, incentives, and processes—may not work well when applied to the management and execution of systematic experimentation, which is, by nature, capital inefficient.
- Experimentation, when done right, is chaotic, natural, and messy—not hierarchical, planned, or objective driven.

It's that last lesson that may be the hardest to apply. It's not practical to manage a company without objectives.

Let's consider again how learning (a.k.a. evolution) happens in the Amazon. Evolution in the Amazon is unmanaged—it's not a top-down, hierarchical, or planned exercise. But it is not a process without constraints. Natural experimentation in the form of mutation is limited by how many resources organisms can access to grow and thrive, and competition determines which organisms are successful. Evolution has not resulted in polar bears or penguins in the Amazon because of constraints.

It is essential that organizations understand and clearly delineate the constraints that determine what kind of experimentation the team will pursue: how much, when, and how.

Experiments, when properly designed and executed, are like call options on a range of future possibilities. They help the organization learn and develop strategic optionality. This does not mean the organization should make a bet in every domain. Trying to reduce risk that way makes it nearly impossible for the company to achieve a big win and locks in the certainty of many failures. Variance is good, but only to a degree. Jack Welch would have been more correct if he had declared, "*unconstrained* variance is evil."

In the reality of an organization, the leadership team risks being spread too thin across too many bets if experimentation is not designed with a link to strategy or constraints. Leaders must set guidelines for where they choose to experiment. Will the organization rely on a strategy of three-pointers? Or take more shots from inside the paint? Is the organization better at one or the other?

Innovation success depends on being very good at selecting which experiments to run—at determining how to manage and allocate limited resources against an almost unlimited set of possible experiments.

Defining the boundaries

Years ago I worked in a corporate innovation group within a global medical diagnostics firm. The company had a business unit that fit the classical definition of a "cash cow," generating profits that subsidized other operating businesses and innovation efforts. The company's vast resources enabled it to do almost anything, which was a challenge for our small innovation team. Should we build software businesses? Or focus on devices? How much of our efforts should be directed toward improving efficiency in the core business? How much focus on building new services for new customers? How far could we stray from healthcare? At a certain point, the choices became almost paralyzing. A mental experiment became a useful filter: if it were obvious that opening ice cream parlors would produce a return above the company's cost of capital, should we open ice cream parlors?

The answer to the question is no, a medical diagnostics company should not open ice cream parlors. Ice cream parlors were not a strategic fit for the company, meaning the opportunity—even if it were a certain thing in the short run—would not capitalize on any of the company's competencies to create lasting advantage. Even if the company's strategy was hard for executives to articulate with precision, it was clear *some things* were out of bounds. In the absence of a clearly articulated corporate strategy, innovation teams should not have to feel their way in the dark, running experiments internally and externally, and returning to the executive team periodically to determine whether the results are within or outside of strategic bounds. It is better to set the bounds up front. Doing so is a far better use of resources, or operating within a world of limited constraints.

The R&D leaders of a global consumer packaged goods firm faced a similar challenge to the one we faced at the medical diagnostics company. Their company was generating enough revenue and free cash flow to enter just about any new industry, market, or geography. There were very few constraints on the R&D team's ability to explore new technologies and product ideas that could propel the firm's growth. This freedom presented profound challenges to the company because effective strategy requires hard decisions. The firm hired my colleagues and me to develop a road map for the R&D team to help them determine what was in and out of bounds.

We decided to approach the ambiguous problem by analyzing the company's customers and their "jobs to be done," or problems for which the customers might "hire" the firm and its products. We categorized the jobs to be done in three broad categories: (1) help me care for my things, (2) help me care for my loved ones, and (3) help me care for myself. Within those broad categories, we identified over seventy secondary jobs to be done that were important and unlikely to be deprioritized by consumers in the future. Next, we mapped a range of technologies for which the firm had expertise or meaningful access to expertise and rated each technology's applicability to the different consumer jobs to be done. We identified "hot spots," where a specific technology could believably address a job to be done (example: using sound waves to sanitize a sink).

Using this method, we defined a broad set of constraints and formed the foundation of a product road map and research strategy. Opening ice cream parlors was not on the priority list; the company had no believable path to relative advantage. But new technologies for preventing elderly parents' bedsores were squarely in range, even if outside the set of products the company was producing at the time. With the constraints properly defined, the R&D team was positioned to prioritize and select experiments that were in line with firm strategy, but they were also capable of challenging status quo beliefs and approaches, of uncovering novelty and surprise.

Innovation is unlikely to succeed if the strategic bounds are not established and agreed upon. An organization's leaders must determine where the organization will play and how it will win. All good strategies are controversial because they represent real choices. Hard choices. Throwing a bunch of spaghetti against the wall to see what sticks is not a strategy. Yes, innovators should seek novelty, but within the constraints of the organization's available resources and stated strategy. Innovators should understand the strategy and ensure their activities are aligned with it. Conversely, the organization should broadly understand how innovators' efforts are critical to the future success of the organization and not merely ancillary or complementary to it. If innovators' experiments are not perceived as critical to the future success of the organization, they will not receive the resources they need, including the benefit of time required to produce results.

Very few large organizations have a well-articulated and widely understood strategy—at least a strategy that most employees or participants in an organization can correctly articulate. Fewer organizations still have a smart strategy. In this vacuum, innovators must still innovate, but their chance of success is diminished. Without a clearly articulated strategy, innovators may need to crystalize the implied strategy—including the bounds of where to play—by defining plausible (if not likely) scenarios and using those scenarios as a guide for where to look for innovation and opportunity. Experiments, if properly designed and executed, can be defined as strategic hedges and options in the face of these scenarios, which then create momentum in their definition for their exploration.[9]

Experiments can be as simple as a phone call with an expert or as elaborate as launching a new business. In each case, having a properly defined hypothesis, parameters for the experiment, and a carefully executed plan will ensure the experiment produces learning. It is easy to justify the results of a failed experiment if the plan wasn't established with clarity up front.

When I was a student in business school, a friend and I launched a startup designed to help commercial mold remediators more easily remove mold from buildings. The key to our approach was an innovative technology for generating chlorine dioxide, a gas known to destroy mold at the cellular level. We didn't get very far. For the business to be successful, we believed the technology had to achieve 100 percent kill rates across every major form of mold. So we ran an experiment. We obtained samples of moldy drywall from commercial demolition projects and placed the drywall inside of sealed containers where we could apply our chlorine dioxide gas over a sufficient period to kill the mold, mimicking conditions that might exist inside a structure. We sent the treated drywall off to a lab for testing and received the test results on graduation day. We printed the results in the computer lab and reviewed the results together as we walked, wearing graduation caps and gowns, to our commencement ceremony.

To our great dismay, the results were not as good as we had hoped: the technology was successful in killing every important type of mold at 100 percent except one, for which it only achieved a 98 percent kill rate. This result didn't cross the threshold we had established before running the experiment, so we decided to stick to our standards and abandon the business. We could have pivoted into a consumer application, but we had also decided the business only made sense for us as a professional, not consumer, endeavor. The experiment worked in that we learned and acted on the results, and each of us quickly found "real jobs," but the missed threshold was a disappointment! Holding to predetermined success metrics is key to running (and learning from) effective experiments.

Options

When considering which experiments to pursue, it is better to consider the value of experiments as options: relative value is more important than real value. The most valuable experiments are those that are likely to create findings that lead to more experiments, that generate findings that challenge the status quo—within strategic constraints. Experiments that confirm what the organization already knows are not relatively valuable and are usually a waste of time and resources. Experiments performed externally through the vehicle of startups and with a system of governance, incentives, talent, and processes optimized for learning are far more likely to produce surprising results that challenge existing thinking. Experiments performed internally using the systems the corporation has optimized for scaled execution of its core business are more likely to confirm what the organization already believes to be true. If learning and optionality are the prime objectives for innovation teams, corporations would benefit from running more experiments at the margins (at the level of individual cells or organisms), and in the world of business, startups do this exceptionally well.

The level of investment in experiments and the proper forum and structure for those experiments depend on how much innovation an organization needs and how soon it needs it. If a corporation needs a lot of innovation and needs it now, a large-scale acquisition may be the most efficient path to transformation. On the other hand, if there is time to learn, then partnerships, external venture investments, and new venture building—where the outcome may not be evident for years—can be appropriate tools. When it comes to transformative innovation, leaders must set specific strategic guidelines and boundaries for experimentation, then determine how to run as many experiments as possible at the lowest possible cost within those guidelines and within the bounds of constraints like time and capital.

Since Clayton Christensen introduced the concept of the innovator's dilemma in 1997, corporations have been experimenting in earnest with methods for launching new ventures and products. New ventures are a specific form of elaborate experimentation, and they can be operated inside the corporation or outside it as an independent company. Truly transformative ventures are nearly impossible to launch internally because they are fundamentally learning challenges, not execution challenges, and as this book has shown, scaled organizations are optimized for execution, not learning. When transformative ventures don't directly threaten the core business, they are often smothered by attention, with everyone inside the corporation wanting to lay claim to the venture's hoped-for success. Increasingly, corporations are experimenting with ways to run venture-building experiments outside the corporation, with incentives, governance, talent, and processes designed and optimized for learning challenges.

How should a corporation choose between an internal or external path for the launch of a new venture? The short answer is that the corporation should choose the path most likely to create the most value in the least amount of time, but that is easier said than done. In reality, most of the innovation ideas a corporation entertains are sustaining to the core, and they should be executed inside the core business under full control of the corporation, even if a new venture is required.

Here's a quick heuristic: If you can build a forecast of first-year financial results for a new business concept with a high degree of confidence, you should likely launch the idea inside of a corporation. If you can predict what is likely to happen, you're probably facing an execution challenge, and the corporation is designed to run and succeed with execution experiments. You know what needs to be done, and you should go do it.

When you're dealing primarily with a learning challenge, the new venture will have a much better chance of success if launched externally, with limited control from the corporation. If you understand the problem but aren't yet confident in the solution, an externally launched venture will likely have the advantage. While scaled corporations are optimized for execution, independent startups are optimized for learning. They are capital inefficient in the near term by design so that they can generate insights that create long-term, outsized outcomes.

Another quick test: If an idea is strategically critical— meaning the future of the corporation depends on the new venture's success—launch it internally. You want to control the outcome carefully. If, on the other hand, the idea is merely strategically "interesting"—something the corporation would benefit from understanding better—then launch externally. You don't want your core team distracted by the new ventures, and you'll learn faster by watching well-incentivized founders run the venture with limited or no strategic constraints imposed by the corporation.

There is tremendous value to be created and captured in building new ventures, and corporations have dramatic advantages over independently launched startups. The trick is to properly structure and manage the incentives and governance, appropriately matching them to the needs of the new venture. External launch should be a go-to tool in every corporate innovator's toolkit; it is among the most successful solutions to the innovator's dilemma.

Internal versus External Venture?
Ask: Which route will create the most value
in the least amount of time?

LAUNCH INTERNALLY, IF:	LAUNCH EXTERNALLY, IF:
There are **more knowns than unknowns**; execution is initially more important than learning	There are more unknowns than knowns; **learning is initially more important than execution**
Moving at SCALE matters more than moving FAST in the beginning	**Moving fast matters more** than moving at scale in the beginning
Close integration with the core will be required (e.g., brand, technology, sales)	The business model or customers are **different from the core's; the venture may even compete**
Internal expertise is more relevant and valuable; internal talent, capital, and resources are sufficient	**External capability or expertise is more relevant and valuable**; outside entrepreneurs and investors can accelerate
The venture is strategically critical; the future of the core depends on the venture's success	The venture is strategically interesting, but not critical (at least yet); **optionality is a key objective**

Source: High Alpha Innovation

When designing experiments, it is important to match the level of investment and experiment fidelity to the degree of confidence. Corporations, in their quest for safety, will always seek to acquire as much information as possible before making a decision or taking action. In the realm of innovation, data very often doesn't exist (yet); the innovator must take *action* to create the data with which he or she can make better decisions. When confidence is low, a quick phone call with an expert might be a viable form of experiment that creates enough data to take the next step (likely a more in-depth experiment). When confidence is high, a more elaborate experiment, like the launch of a new venture, may be appropriate.

In the 2019 film *Ford v Ferrari,* there's an instructive scene in which engineers from Ford Motor Company are collaborating with the team from a much smaller enterprise, Shelby American, to test a new model of the Ford GT40 on the racetrack in the 1960s. Ford, with ample resources and a desire to collect as much data as possible, places a computer with many sensors in the car to monitor its performance. The driver, Ken Miles, no fan of corporate stodginess, gets frustrated with the space the computer requires inside the car, and pulls the computer out, wires and all, to the dismay of the Ford engineers. Instead, the Shelby team covers the car with strips of yarn and masking tape and uses the cheap "sensors" to monitor airflow across the outside of the vehicle. The yarn is used to discover significant drag on the vehicle at racing speed, and the joint team goes on to make design changes to the vehicle that result in a much faster car. The scene is a perfect demonstration of the different approaches to experimentation and learning that startups and large corporations are designed for and the importance of matching experiment fidelity to confidence.

Fluent in CFO speak

When experiments are aligned with strategy, producing sufficient insights to deliver on objectives, and being executed efficiently, an organization's experiment engine is working. Metrics can be used to monitor the effectiveness of experiments in all three dimensions: alignment, sufficiency, and efficiency. Changes can be made along all three dimensions to better tune the program.

The challenge of such a systematic approach to experimentation is that the immediate results the system produces are learning and optionality, but what the CFO needs is predictable and near-term financial results. As discussed earlier in this book, scaled corporations are optimized for near-term return on investment. It is generally hard to access funding for innovation inside of large organizations because the outcomes are uncertain, and the requests compete with alternative uses where the return on investment is predictable, known, and understood.

CFOs care about two things: (1) how much cash the company generates (earnings) and (2) how much the company is worth (multiple). Earnings and multiple are the metrics that determine the stock price for publicly traded companies. Innovation leaders can directly impact both metrics through their activities, including through external experimentation.

Innovation leaders can remove the negative impact on earnings that innovation investment normally has by moving innovation into new standalone ventures, turning innovation activity into a balance sheet investment rather than an operating expense. More importantly, by experimenting actively in adjacent and transformative spaces where multiples are higher demonstrating real traction through new ventures in those domains, innovation leaders can change the narrative of the company and its public perception, all while learning and creating long-term strategic optionality for the business.

As previously discussed, not every innovation opportunity has exponential growth potential and should be spun out of the company. Startup creation works best on transformational opportunities that may compete against the core business (or disrupt it) and where strategic alignment may not be certain.

Innovation is best funded as an operating expense when the ideas are close to the core business. This type of innovation requires capital that is impatient. When you're innovating close to the core you can compete for budget with sure-thing requests like marketing spend. Like the operating business, this type of innovation is capital efficient. A negative short-term drag on earnings is acceptable because the time to payback is short.

On the other hand, innovation is better funded from the balance sheet when it challenges or looks very different from the core business. These kinds of innovation need patient capital that can wait longer for returns. These kinds of innovation require a longer payback period because so much learning is involved; efficiency comes later. Experiments with these kinds of innovation are best executed in new ventures and funded as balance sheet investments, with no negative impact on earnings. When done properly, this approach can even leverage other investors' capital and expertise. It's a fast and inexpensive way to learn. Importantly, it's predictable in its own way.

Downside risk is capped in the investment amount, without a ceiling on upside potential. The approach enables the team that manages the core business to remain focused without distraction. The new venture's success or failure is up to the founding team in that venture, and when done properly, they don't require access to the core business's systems of incentives, talent, or governance.

If there's a single piece of advice large companies should consider when launching external ventures, it's this: Don't constrain a new venture's strategic or financial options. Take a minority stake in the new business initially, with the option to increase the corporation's stake over time. The goal is to generate learning and optionality, not safety. If you truly want insights and surprises, incentivize world-class entrepreneurs to move quickly and with relative autonomy. You usually can't be both rich and king. Allowing a venture more freedom increases its chance to succeed (and bring in riches)—that's much better than being in total control of something that fails. Properly incentivized and structured startups are a cheap form of experiment for large corporations.

The takeaway? Run more experiments: fast, cheap, and weird.

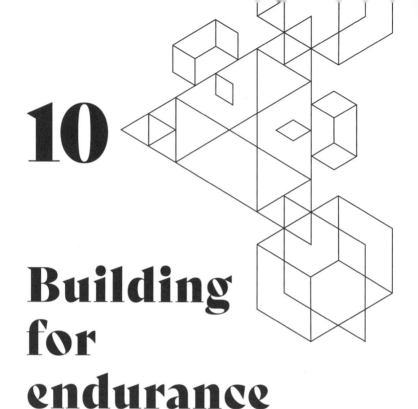

10

Building for endurance

Long-term thinking creates lasting competitive advantage and progress.

When Birkenstock, the famous manufacturer of footwear, executed its initial public offering in late 2023, the market valued the company at more than $7 billion.

Birkenstock's march to IPO was long; the company's roots go back to its founding in 1774 by Johann Adam Birkenstock in Langen-Bergheim, Germany. Over 250 years of operation, the business endured much, surviving world wars, political upheaval, and dramatic changes in fashion.

According to its CEO at the time of the IPO, Birkenstock "remain[ed] empowered by a youthful energy level, with all the freshness and creative versatility of an inspired Silicon Valley startup." He went on to say that it retained "the original spirit of [its] forefathers who laid the foundation of a global business that is more relevant than ever before." At the time of its IPO, the company was generating over $1 billion in annual revenue.

Although the CEO may believe Birkenstock to be "fresh," it is quite old, but far from the oldest corporation in existence. Compared with most corporations whose life spans are shrinking on average, Birkenstock is certainly an outlier.

My former colleagues at consulting firm Innosight do a study every few years looking at the average duration of companies on the S&P 500, and they've found that company life spans are contracting: from forty years in the 1960s to about half that in the 2020s.[1] Technology-enabled decentralization is making it harder for centralized corporations to innovate faster than the market and to compete with upstarts.

Not only are companies dying earlier on average, but many publicly traded companies aren't even creating value for their owners when they are operating. Hendrik Bessembinder, a professor of finance at Arizona State University, published a study in 2023 on the prior one hundred years of performance for public companies. He found that nearly 60 percent of them failed to outperform one-month Treasury bills, a proxy for the risk-free rate of capital.[2]

It gets worse: Bessembinder also found that only 2 percent of companies were responsible for more than 90 percent of the aggregate net wealth creation in the US stock market.

In 2013, Paul Kedrosky of the Ewing Marion Kauffman Foundation found that in any given year in the United States, entrepreneurs launch roughly 552,000 companies, yet only 125–250 of those will ever reach $100 million in revenue.[3] Most companies are not growth firms and never begin with a goal to reach such lofty revenue numbers, but still, the number is stark: very few companies ever reach escape velocity.

The point? Building companies with enduring impact is incredibly difficult and rare. The world needs more entrepreneurs, and it needs more of them to succeed at what they do. Enduring companies are interesting because they are outliers that create long cycles over which they can solve problems and impact the world.

A fifteen-century run

The most enduring company in the world was founded one hundred years after the fall of the Roman Empire and didn't succumb to acquisition until the start of the twenty-first century. Here's the remarkable story.

In AD 578, a Japanese prince invited a Korean carpenter named Kongō Shikō to construct Shitennō-ji, the "Temple of the Four Heavenly Kings," in Osaka, Japan. The temple is still standing today, having been carefully maintained and rebuilt over time. The company that Kongō Shikō launched in Japan to manage the temple's construction endured for fifteen centuries. Like the temple itself, the company was prudently maintained by many generations of caretakers before collapsing under a significant debt load and slowing demand for its services. Until its 2006 acquisition by the Takamatsu Construction Group, Kongō Gumi Co., Ltd. was the world's oldest continually operating company.

Over its history, the construction company worked primarily on the design, building, and restoration of shrines, temples, and other cultural heritage sites. For nearly all that time, up through its eventual acquisition, the company was owned and guided by a single family. A ten-foot-long scroll from the seventeenth century lists the names of every generation of company leaders, tracing its management back to the beginning in the sixth century. Following tradition, sons-in-law adopted the Kongō family name when there was no son to take the helm. Eventually, daughters were also allowed to run the business.

The company exhibited flexibility in how it chose its leaders, selecting the son who showed the most potential to succeed in the job rather than simply defaulting to the rule of primogeniture. Masakazu Kongō, the last member of the family to lead the company in its independent state, credited that flexibility for the company's ability to endure so long.

Kongō Gumi's durability was also due in part to the company's link to Buddhism; the religion had staying power, and Kongō Gumi was in business to create physical structures to enable its practice. As long as there was Buddhism and its millions of adherents in Japan, there would be a need for the company's temples and shrines.

The company survived some trying times, including changes in government. During the Meiji Restoration in the nineteenth century, Kongō Gumi lost its government subsidies and had to begin building commercial buildings for the first time. Governments, technologies, people, and building practices came and went over the centuries, but during this time, temple construction remained the core business and contributed 80 percent of the company's $67.6 million in revenue in 2004.[4]

It's hard to imagine the weight of responsibility that Masakazu Kongō, the final leader in the long family line, must have felt when the company began faltering under his watch. In the early 1990s, a real estate crash lowered the value of assets the company used to secure loans, and the debt burden became difficult to manage. Kongō Gumi was not the only construction company in Japan experiencing debt woes at the time. The fatal blow, however, was a reduction in contributions to temples in Japan, resulting in a drop in demand for temple construction and repair.

By 2004, revenues were down 35 percent from their peak. Masakazu Kongō laid off employees and tried to cut costs, but the efforts were not enough to save the company from a sale. The company's debt had increased to $343 million, and there was simply no way to service that level of debt anymore. In January 2006, Takamatsu Construction Group, a large Japanese construction company, acquired Kongō Gumi, and the oldest company in the world became a subsidiary.

While the demise of Kongō Gumi is instructive, its endurance is much more enlightening. It's hard to apply specific lessons from this unique company universally across institutions, but there are some insights to consider, and when the company is compared against other long-lived institutions, some patterns begin to emerge.

For most companies, endurance is a better goal than short-term profit maximization. If cash flow *is* the most important measure of a company's success, sustained cash flow generation over centuries, even if at a meager rate annually, is likely more desirable than a short-term spike and crash. Total volume under the profit curve over a long period is more important than the peak in any single quarter or year.

Business schools teach students that profitability, or ROIC, is the most important measure of a company's success, while underemphasizing the time dimension that must be factored into that measure to understand it correctly. Profitability is usually measured in quarterly or annual increments, for no reason other than such timing aligns with attention spans and regulatory requirements. Think how differently the world would operate if profitability were measured over ten- or one-hundred-year increments. Durability should matter when accounting for an institution's success.

The writer James Carse famously described "infinite games," meaning games where the objective is to be able to continue playing for as long as possible. He contrasted this with "finite games," in which there's a clear ending and someone is declared the winner.[5] Most of the time—although not always—the point of business is to endure and thereby maximize value creation and impact.

Game theory teaches us that when we play finite games, we optimize for our own outcome because there is no threat of repercussion. When we play infinite games, we must optimize for all stakeholders to keep playing. Too many forget that business is better played as an infinite game.

Enduring institutions

The list of institutions founded before AD 1100 that have been in continuous operation is longer than one might suspect:

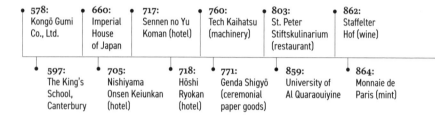

578: Kongō Gumi Co., Ltd.	660: Imperial House of Japan	717: Sennen no Yu Koman (hotel)	760: Tech Kaihatsu (machinery)	803: St. Peter Stiftskulinarium (restaurant)	862: Staffelter Hof (wine)
597: The King's School, Canterbury	705: Nishiyama Onsen Keiunkan (hotel)	718: Hōshi Ryokan (hotel)	771: Genda Shigyō (ceremonial paper goods)	859: University of Al Quaraouiyine	864: Monnaie de Paris (mint)

Not long after William the Conqueror won the Battle of Hastings in 1066, students began gathering in Oxford, England, to study and learn. Over time the institution grew, becoming more established and important. Visitors and students today will likely be surprised at how much tradition endures in the institution. Somehow, Oxford (like many other universities) has learned how to balance adherence to tradition with constant refreshing and renewal.

For example: the university's graduation ceremonies are still held in Latin. The format of the program has remained

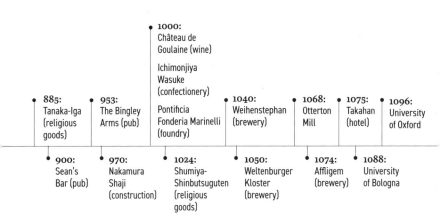

885:
Tanaka-Iga
(religious
goods)

900:
Sean's
Bar (pub)

953:
The Bingley
Arms (pub)

970:
Nakamura
Shaji
(construction)

1000:
Château de
Goulaine (wine)

Ichimonjiya
Wasuke
(confectionery)

Pontificia
Fonderia Marinelli
(foundry)

1024:
Shumiya-
Shinbutsuguten
(religious
goods)

1040:
Weihenstephan
(brewery)

1050:
Weltenburger
Kloster
(brewery)

1068:
Otterton
Mill

1074:
Affligem
(brewery)

1075:
Takahan
(hotel)

1088:
University
of Bologna

1096:
University
of Oxford

mostly unchanged for over 800 years. True, there have been mild changes over the centuries, but changes have tended to be cosmetic. For a long time, the ceremonies were laborious affairs, requiring many hours to complete, as each graduate had to be presented and walked before the audience individually. Sometime in the last 150 years, an innovation occurred that allowed five graduates to be presented at a time (each holding a finger of the proctor's hand, while before only one graduate could hold the proctor's hand at a time), thus speeding up the service by a factor of five. While this innovation was surely welcomed and appreciated when it was incorporated, other traditions—like the reading in Latin—have remained unchanged. Indeed, much of the symbolism has been completely lost to time: participants have no idea why they're doing or saying the things they do and say in the ceremony. The traditions continue, however, because participants feel compelled to perpetuate them; the traditions, even if the original meaning is unknown, bind the participants to those who have gone before. Tradition carries weight and provides meaning. And so tradition dictates the order of the ceremony, the handshakes, the words participants say, even the specific clothing that must be worn. And the University of Oxford endures.

There is much that is in constant flux at the university. Every four years or so, the student body is replaced, and the institution has to attract an entirely new set of customers. True, the tradition and reputation of the institution carry a lot of weight, but course offerings, methods of teaching, and social elements of the experience change all the time. It is also easy to imagine how the institution might squander its appeal through a failure to adapt; many institutions have gone that way before.

In 1920, for example, Oxford thankfully permitted women to begin taking degrees at the university, thus doubling the potential market for the university's offerings. (This idea had been rejected in 1909 as being far too radical.[6]) It wasn't until 1974, however, that five all-male undergraduate colleges—Brasenose, Jesus, Wadham, Hertford, and St. Catherine's—began accepting women for the first time. At the same time, Greek was dropped as a compulsory element of the examination the university gave to all entering students. Not all schools in Britain taught Greek at the time, so dropping this requirement similarly expanded the number of applicants who might consider enrolling at the university.

Many degree titles at the university date from the Middle Ages, and the system remains confusing to the uninitiated. But the content of those degree programs has changed drastically over time. In the medieval period, students at Oxford studied the seven liberal arts: grammar, rhetoric, dialectic, arithmetic, geometry, music, and astronomy. Six years of study were required to earn a Bachelor of Arts degree. Later, the university expanded its curriculum to include subjects such as Greek, Hebrew, and modern languages. Mathematics and natural sciences became more prominent, and the university began awarding degrees in medicine and law.

University leaders radically overhauled the curriculum in the nineteenth century, and that evolution continued into the twentieth. Today, Oxford offers a wide array of degree programs and many interdisciplinary programs of study. What has remained unchanged is the university's rigor and commitment to excellence no matter the subject. So, while much is different, there are elements of the institution that are unlikely to ever change. This helps the institution adapt and endure. The institution has decided—organically—what can change and what must not.

Kongō Gumi and the University of Oxford are very different institutions, with no commonality in their mission or purpose. But both lasted (and in the case of Oxford, continue to thrive) for a very long time. The list of long-lived institutions is interesting for its diversity as much as for its blandness. It seems helpful to have started in Japan, which accounts for far more of the world's long-lived institutions than any other region. (We'll come back to that.)

If one skips ahead several centuries, many companies that American consumers are familiar with were founded in the late eighteenth or early nineteenth century and are still in operation today, like Birkenstock. For example:

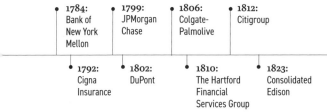

1784:
Bank of
New York
Mellon

1792:
Cigna
Insurance

1799:
JPMorgan
Chase

1802:
DuPont

1806:
Colgate-
Palmolive

1810:
The Hartford
Financial
Services Group

1812:
Citigroup

1823:
Consolidated
Edison

Common patterns emerge in this list of "baby" companies that are also relevant to the list of institutions created before AD 1100. While there are clear and obvious exceptions, for the most part, long-lived institutions seem to exhibit some shared qualities.

Take time to build

Institutions are more likely to endure when their founding requires the efforts of multiple generations. Gothic cathedrals are a good example of this principle. The Reims Cathedral, near where I once lived in France, was built in different iterations over the course of a thousand years. It's where Clovis was baptized and the kings of France were crowned. The generations of craftsmen who worked on the cathedral persisted through major setbacks like fire and wars to get it done. The cathedral was severely damaged during the first World War, and restoration is still ongoing over one hundred years later.

A small group of people can start construction of a cathedral, but a cathedral requires a large group of people, sometimes over hundreds of years, to finish the job.

The multicentury effort creates nearly unstoppable momentum over time. While the effort of a single person, executed during that person's lifetime, is easy to forget and discard, the work of generations is hard to drop. Momentum builds and carries. Today, citizens and governments in Europe go to extraordinary lengths to preserve their cathedrals, even though religious adherence is waning.

The lesson? Don't run faster than you can handle. It's fine to take time if your financing structure allows for it. Birkenstock took 250 years to get to $1 billion in revenue! Consider that it may take generations of leaders to reach your company's ultimate objectives. If those objectives are meaningful and important enough, a long timeline is desirable and admirable. I'm not suggesting you should be modest in your objectives—the builders of the cathedral in Reims certainly were not. I'm suggesting that you should be audacious in your objectives and conservative in your timelines. Or, as John D. Rockefeller told his son, "Plan boldly and implement carefully."[7]

Help society win

Long-lived institutions create more than they consume. Contrary to popular wisdom, they don't seek to maximize profitability in the short term, and they don't pursue or achieve monopoly status. Instead, they earn "enough" to maintain their presence in a market and to remain hard to kill as a result; they are not greedy. In fact, most of the long-lived institutions founded before the eighteenth century have never grown larger than three hundred employees.

Contrast this with the declining life spans of today's newer companies, which rise and fall quickly as they seek to maximize near-term profitability and rapid growth at nearly any cost. Companies that maximize short-term profits tend to burn brightly and quickly like a meteor shooting across the sky. Enduring institutions are more like stars, steady in the sky, even if their light is relatively dim. For enduring institutions, growth is unhurried and not the primary objective.

In contrast, organizations that succeed in capturing an outsized allocation of value in a market tend to not last long. Society eventually rejects them. There are no monopolies on the list of institutions founded before the year 1100. Monopolies don't endure.

Since over half the world's companies that have lasted more than two hundred years are based in Japan, it's worth considering what is going on there. There are many possible reasons why Japan has a claim to so many long-lived companies. One theory is the principle of *sanpo yoshi*, roughly translated as "three-way satisfaction."

In the nineteenth century, a small group of villagers began crisscrossing Japan selling mosquito nets, cloth, medicine, and other goods from their native Omi region. These traveling merchants, known as the Omi Shonin, eventually expanded their operations and created a national network of small shops up and down Japan, becoming one of the most successful and influential merchant groups in the country.

Their origins strongly influenced the way they did business. For the traveling Omi Shonin to be successful, they had to build long-term, trusting relationships with the communities in which they operated. They knew their success depended on the good graces of their customers, so the Omi Shonin emphasized their positive impact on the communities in which they worked, sponsoring construction of schools, bridges, and shrines, and sometimes paying bills for impoverished families.

They built for the long run and viewed investment and impact in the community as a way to ensure resilience in their business and profits. They made sure their business operations were good for them, good for their customers, and good for the society in which they operated: three-way satisfaction. Near-term ROIC was not the sole measure of success, and society determined it was good for the Omi Shonin to continue to be in business.

Long-lasting institutions are often driven by a mission that is considered more significant than the institution itself. Oxford University is a perfect example of this. Many of the long-lived institutions are closely linked to religious observance. Kongō Gumi focused on temple construction and maintenance, and it thrived as long as Buddhists made donations.

A more exhaustive list of enduring institutions would include many religious orders for which the organization itself is a means to a greater end for those who perpetuate its existence. At some point, for many of the most enduring institutions, propagation of the institution to maintain an unbroken chain of operation sometimes takes over as a version of a larger mission. Continuance of the organization is viewed by participants as a form of service to those who came before and those who are yet to come.

The important lesson? If you're building a company, make sure your mission matters and has a link to societal benefit that is obvious. Companies persist at society's pleasure.

Operate in stable industries

In the modern world we can use our phones to track the location of our teenagers when they're out late on a Saturday night. Our ancestors in the seventeenth century didn't have this luxury.

A much trickier problem for them was calculating their location when out at sea, especially after weeks of sailing. Many sailors died over the centuries because there was not a good way to calculate longitude until the eighteenth century, when the British Parliament initiated the Longitude Act, with the help of Sir Isaac Newton and Edmond Halley, to spur solutions to the problem.

Before the longitude problem was solved, the best one could do with confidence was to calculate latitude using a tool called an astrolabe. Mariners used astrolabes all the way back to the Roman Empire, and likely centuries before. Astrolabes helped operators triangulate time and location from the position of the stars or sun and were a popular tool throughout the world up until the eighteenth century. They were particularly relied upon in the Islamic world for their ability to help point believers to Mecca and track the proper times for prayers.

Astrolabes are no longer in widespread use, although one might claim the phones we carry in our pockets are a modern version. There are no astrolabe manufacturers anymore, and there are no enduring astrolabe companies. The market for astrolabes was consistent for many centuries, and then it evaporated.

Similarly, modern companies focused on the manufacture of calculators will not endure for centuries to come unless they're able to pivot into a more stable space. Enduring institutions exist in strong ecosystems, focused on slowly or never-changing customer needs. If you want to build an enduring institution, your chance of success may be greater if you open a small hotel or restaurant than if you manufacture cars. This is ironic; the barriers to entry in these enduring industries tend to be low. Perhaps robust competition breeds strength and endurance.

The oldest limited liability corporation in the world, a Swedish company called Stora Enso, was founded in 1288 as a copper mine. It pivoted over time to iron mining, then paper and pulp manufacturing. By the 1970s it was almost entirely focused on forestry-related businesses. Most recently it executed a company-wide transformation into sustainable building products. The executive team reached out to the entire employee base and asked for suggestions for new products and services during that transformation. That kind of change is hard. But leaders' willingness to reinvent and humility about the future are what help long-lived institutions endure by pivoting into new spaces when required.

If we consider the list of operating companies founded before AD 1100, we won't see any manufacturers of astrolabes, galleons, or chariots. The companies that endure chose domains that were as relevant one thousand years ago as they are today. If you want to build something that endures, choose a stable, enduring industry in which to build. Or build a company that can pivot and adjust into new, more stable industries over time.

Remember

Enduring companies are very good at remembering what they've learned.

One of the oldest operating clocks in the world can be found at the Salisbury Cathedral in England. The person who maintains the clock is called the "Keeper of the Fabric."

Alexander Rose of the Long Now Foundation has documented how many cathedrals in the United Kingdom employ a person whose title is "Keeper of the Fabric," who is responsible for ensuring the cathedral is well maintained and protected for future generations.[8] This includes overseeing repairs and restoration work, but it also often includes maintaining and sharing the stories of the institution: its history and heritage. These stories become critical in the propagation of these institutions and for the role they play in reinforcing culture while delineating what must be preserved and what can be refreshed or changed over time. Stories, like traditions, endow the institution with weight and importance.

All enduring institutions are successful at preserving and retelling stories to reinforce culture, mission, and devotion. If you're building a company, consider how you document and propagate your founding stories and how knowledge is passed on over time from elders to the newly arrived. Enduring institutions do this proactively and deliberately.

Be fiscally resilient

Companies that last centuries don't gamble with their resources. Times are often challenging for venture-backed startups, and some times are harder than others. "Mass

extinction" events come and go, but hard times create enduring, disciplined companies.

Kongō Gumi survived changes in political regimes, dev-
astation from war, famines, fires, and much more. Ironically,
its eventual demise was self-imposed: it collapsed because
it tried to grow too quickly by taking on debt it ultimately
couldn't repay. Times may be challenging now and then, but
many companies have survived much harder times. Strength
is built through struggle.

In 2022, research firm CB Insights documented the primary reasons startups fail.[9] "Got outcompeted" and "flawed
business model" were among the top reasons cited. There
may be many contributing factors to the failure of companies, but no startup ever failed because the founders didn't
get along or a pivot didn't work. Companies fail for one reason only: they run out of money. If you want your company
to endure, don't run out of money. Of course, that's much
easier said than done!

The world's most enduring institutions are hyperconser-
vative about fiscal matters. They take very little risk. They
can afford to be cautious because they're typically tightly
held and not worried about short-term growth. They're more
interested in operating one hundred years from now than

maximizing profit next quarter. They're more interested in playing an infinite game.

In May 2020, just as the first wave of the COVID-19 pandemic was getting underway, a famous professor in Japan named Toshio Goto surveyed the country's centenarian companies. More than a quarter of the companies said they had enough cash on hand at the time to last for two or more years, with most saving for a rainy day in the belief that a major crisis typically hits about once every ten years. One company, a factory automation business, boasted it could survive for seventeen years without any revenue if it needed to!

Enduring companies are hard to kill. Paul Graham, founder of Y Combinator and successful investor in hundreds of startups, urges founders to make sure their companies are hard to kill by being "cheap to run" and having a mission that attracts believers: "If you're really committed and your startup is cheap to run, you become very hard to kill. . . . If doing good for people gives you a sense of mission that makes you harder to kill, that alone more than compensates for whatever you lose by not choosing a more selfish project."[10]

For startups, being fiscally conservative means keeping the burn rate low and funding operations through revenue as much as possible. It means being slow to hire and creative in acquiring customers. Having a compelling mission is meaningless if a founder can't tell the story of the company in a way that others are inspired to share. Every successful and enduring company has a mission that benefits the society in which it operates.

Reinvent what can change

Companies that endure have a clear sense of what must never change, but they are very good at reinventing everything else, all the time.

The same family has been operating the Hōshi Ryokan, a Japanese inn founded in AD 718, for over 47 generations. At the heart of the hotel is a collection of hot spring baths, reputed to have healing powers. The hotel preserves these hot baths with care and retells legends associated with their creation and use and stories of famous people healed by the waters. The springs are unalterable. In contrast, over the centuries, the hotel has adjusted with the times, changing its methods of operations, its services to guests, and its marketing and sales tactics. The hotel's rooms are modern and comfortably appointed, and the menu is updated regularly to reflect changing tastes. The family managing the hotel has a keen understanding of what cannot change while recognizing that everything else *must* be regularly questioned, reconsidered, and altered.

If you're running a business, what is your north star? What must remain fixed? And what else might, could, or should change over time? At the company I run, High Alpha Innovation, our north star is building startups. At the moment, the venture studio approach we've developed over the last eight years is the most efficient and best way we know to build new companies, but that could change over time. For us, the "how" is subject to change, but the "what" and "why" never are.

When you start a new company, you may think you know a lot about the opportunity in front of you and about your industry, customers, and product. But almost always, when viewed retrospectively, the organization's base of knowledge at the start of anything is very, very small. Over time the base of knowledge can grow significantly, through lots of hard work, mistakes, and success. The base of knowledge expands every time the organization invalidates a hypothesis or when something breaks and the team learns.

Enduring companies are like living organisms that must learn and expand their knowledge base to survive. Too many make the mistake of believing companies are more like machines, with parts that need fixing and updating. Enduring organizations are good at learning and remembering and pivoting when required. Action creates data about the future, and knowledge compounds over time. Long-lived institutions capture and store knowledge, but they also understand what they still need to learn and improve upon and actively run experiments to do so. Those experiments are most effective when done in the service of better understanding and delivering on customer needs.

Obsess over customers

Long-term orientation is inseparable from customer obsession; it is born out of a deep care for customers. This may be the most important characteristic of long-lived companies: they care for their stakeholders—past, present, and future.

Jeff Bezos, founder of Amazon, is undoubtedly one of the most successful entrepreneurs of the twenty-first century. In 2018 he attracted attention and surprise when he told his employees at an all-hands meeting that Amazon would, one day, inevitably fail and go bankrupt. But he also explained that in the meantime, it was the job of Amazon employees to delay the inevitable failure for as long as possible. His instructions for ensuring Amazon survives for a long time? "Obsess over customers."[11]

Organizations that focus on their customers avoid crowds; they more easily move into unexplored spaces where competition is not so cutthroat. More importantly, a focus on customers enables organizations to learn to adapt through constant experimentation. You want to build an enduring company? Build products and a culture that people want.

In a 2008 letter to shareholders, Bezos explained:

> [Amazon's] fundamental approach remains the same. Stay heads down, focused on the long term and obsessed over customers. *Long-term thinking levers our existing abilities and lets us do new things we couldn't otherwise contemplate.* It supports the failure and iteration required for invention, and it frees us to pioneer in unexplored spaces. Seek instant gratification—or the elusive promise of it—and chances are you'll find a crowd there ahead of you. Long-term orientation interacts well with customer obsession. If we can identify a customer need and if we can further develop conviction that that need is meaningful and durable, *our approach permits us to work patiently for multiple years to deliver a solution.* "Working backwards" from customer needs can be contrasted with a "skills-forward" approach where existing skills and competencies are used to drive business opportunities. The skills-forward approach says, "We are really good at X. What else can we do with X?" That's a useful and rewarding business approach.

> However, if used exclusively, the company employing it will never be driven to develop fresh skills. Eventually the existing skills will become outmoded. Working backwards from customer needs often *demands* that we acquire new competencies and exercise new muscles, never mind how uncomfortable and awkward-feeling those first steps might be.[12] (Emphasis added.)

Amazon will ultimately go out of business. It is unlikely to last as long as Kongō Gumi did. Time will tell how successfully the company's employees can delay the inevitable and maximize the organization's impact. What seems obvious, however, is that if the company can remain relentlessly focused on the customer, it will thrive for much longer than competitors do *because most companies don't operate this way.* Amazon is a patient organization, willing to try things that take years to pay off as long as customer satisfaction is the eventual outcome.

Those who change the world for the better build institutions that are mission oriented and optimized for long-term impact while finding new ways to serve the needs of their stakeholders. Again, it becomes clear that the secret to endurance is constant, rapid, and inexpensive experimentation in service of customer needs.

All enduring institutions begin with a single founder, as a startup. The future is not predetermined, and we are all responsible for how it plays out. We should want to be good ancestors and build things that will positively impact the world for centuries to come.

Part Three:

WINNING THE FUTURE

11

The optimists will win

Corporate leaders have reason to be optimistic about their role in creating the future.

The ancient Egyptians began experimenting with the construction of pyramids at a place called Saqqara almost five thousand years ago. The pyramids are still standing, and archaeologists are still discovering new tombs at the site. If you travel to Saqqara, you can see the earliest pyramids and observe how Egyptians tested different materials and techniques as they developed ever more elaborate methods of burial for those whom they revered. The pyramids at Saqqara are the early precursors to the better-known Great Pyramid of Khufu, which was built about two hundred years later. As interesting as the pyramids are for what they teach us about life in ancient Egypt, the everyday items left behind at the site by the thousands of people who lived and worked in the area are far more enlightening. Saqqara has been a rich source for archaeologists to uncover clues about everyday life in ancient Egypt.

Near Saqqara, for example, archaeologists find items like spoons. It's not unusual to find spoons from ancient Egypt, and you can even buy them online if you know where to look. Spoons are one of many inventions from ancient Egypt that we still use today. Cheese was also invented in ancient Egypt, and so were tables, chairs, beds, combs and scissors, wedding rings, and games like hockey and bowling. Ancient Egyptians even invented marshmallows and pies. It's not surprising that we attribute so many inventions to the ancient Egyptians. After all, it was a civilization that endured for more than three thousand years.

What is remarkable is that there were not *more* inventions—that technology did not accelerate faster. Stretched over three thousand years, the list of inventions begins to look rather sparse and advancement relatively slow. An Egyptian born in 2500 BC would have lived a very similar life—with similar culture, clothing, religion, and tools—to an Egyptian born in 500 BC. Why didn't things advance more quickly?

The writer Tim Urban proposed an intriguing thought experiment:

> Imagine taking a time machine back to 1750—a time when the world was in a permanent power outage, long-distance communication meant either yelling

loudly or firing a cannon in the air, and all transportation ran on hay. When you get there, you retrieve a dude, bring him to 2015, and then walk him around and watch him react to everything. It's impossible for us to understand what it would be like for him to see shiny capsules racing by on a highway, talk to people who had been on the other side of the ocean earlier in the day, watch sports that were being played 1,000 miles away, hear a musical performance that happened 50 years ago, and play with [a] magical wizard rectangle that he could use to capture a real-life image or record a living moment, generate a map with a paranormal moving blue dot that shows him where he is, look at someone's face and chat with them even though they're on the other side of the country, and worlds of other inconceivable sorcery. This is all before you show him the internet or explain things like the International Space Station, the Large Hadron Collider, nuclear weapons, or general relativity. This experience for him wouldn't be surprising or shocking or even mind-blowing—those words aren't big enough. He might actually die.[1]

Urban goes on to explain that if you were to go back further in history and take someone from 1500 to 1750, an equivalent time span, the individual from 1500 would not be very surprised by the world of 1750. The clothing might look different, but the tools and technologies, culture, and things generally would look very familiar. Urban proposed that for someone to be so surprised by the world of 1750 that they'd "die on the spot," you might have to go back as far as 12,000 BC to find a time traveler, back to the time of the first Agricultural Revolution that gave rise to the first cities. For someone from 12,000 BC to find a time traveler who would die upon seeing the world at that time, that individual might have to go back as far as 100,000 BC, when people were just starting to use fire.

Urban calls these spans of time "Die Progress Units" and suggests that the time spans are shrinking and that this is a sign the pace of invention is accelerating. Pretty soon, a Die Progress Unit might be only fifty years instead of two hundred or three hundred. With the acceleration of artificial intelligence, that span could shorten drastically.

While this thought experiment is somewhat tongue in cheek, it makes a relevant and useful point. Our lives are different from the lives of our ancestors who lived only 250 years ago, let alone thousands of years ago in places like ancient Rome or Egypt or 14,000 years ago when the first cities were being built. Why does invention and technology advance so much faster today than it did in the past? Why did technology advance so slowly in ancient Egypt? And what can we do to ensure progress continues to move at a beneficial pace?

Enablers of innovation

There are two primary factors that determine the pace of innovation:

- *Prevalence of technology building blocks*: access to inventions makes it easier for people to mash together ideas and create more inventions.
- *Ease of idea exchange:* increased connectivity leads to an increased exchange of ideas and therefore more and better ideas.

In the past there was a relative lack of exchange and commerce, which led to a slow exchange of ideas. In places like ancient Egypt, there were few technology building blocks. Egyptians had to invent spoons! They had to create the foundation from scratch, and advances came more slowly than they do today. We are living in an unprecedented age of abundance thanks to innovation that is the result of prevalent communication and access to technology building blocks.

Global communication is already effectively free, the first of three enabling and foundational technologies to become widely accessible. Computational power and energy are similarly trending toward free. The cost of computing power as measured by processing speed per dollar has dropped steeply and steadily since the early days of the microprocessor. The cost of energy, when measured across centuries, is on a steady downward decline. In 1996 future Nobel laureate William Nordhaus showed that the price of light per 1,000 lumens was $785 in 1800 and 23 cents in 1992.[2] While fusion technology is far from economically viable right now, scientists have demonstrated that it is at least physically possible in a controlled environment. It is not crazy to think that someone reading this book in a few decades will be doing so on a device powered by unlimited, nearly free energy generated by a fusion reactor. When communication, computational intelligence, and energy are all free and widely available, innovation should progress exponentially faster: more ideas, more sharing of them, at lower cost.

Free and boundless communication

We are living in a great natural experiment: We are more connected than ever, to an extent that was unimaginable not long ago. We do not yet understand what the long-term effects will be, but we are seeing some of them manifest already in the increased power of individuals and decreased relative effectiveness of institutions.

When I was growing up in the 1980s, the phone company charged extra fees for "long-distance" calls and calculated those fees by the minute. One had to be careful not to dial the wrong number! Communication is now effectively free for almost everyone, anywhere in the world, and this is a dramatic (if underappreciated) change in the human condition.

In the early days of commercial trading across oceans, merchants would have to travel by boat from one continent to another simply to obtain price updates. Such communication was extremely expensive and inefficient; the transaction costs were outrageously high for a merchant in Europe who wanted pepper from India. Some of these costs carried into relatively modern times. Let's imagine you lived in New York City in the 1860s and wanted to have a conversation with someone in California. One way to do that would be to pay someone about $20,000 in 2020 dollars to drive you across the country in a stagecoach or wagon, which could take many months. At the end of your journey you'd be in California and finally able to deliver your message in person. Then you'd have to find more money and time for the return trip.

Eventually, telephones were invented to make things easier. But even phones were still relatively expensive in the beginning. In 1915, a ten-minute call across the country cost the equivalent of $2,000 in 2021 dollars. That price dropped precipitously over the years. So much so that in 2006 the FCC stopped tracking the price of cross-country calls as it approached zero. Now we don't think anything of a video call anywhere in the world. It's effectively free for most of us.

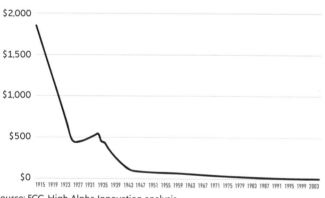

What Exponential Improvement Looks Like
The Cost of a 10-Minute Call, NYC to LA, in 2021 Dollars

Source: FCC, High Alpha Innovation analysis

Collision and exchange of ideas are what lead to new ideas. Human beings learn skills from each other by copying individuals they admire, and they innovate by making mistakes or mutations that are occasionally improvements. That is how culture evolves. *The bigger the connected population and the more skilled the teachers, the higher the probability of productive collisions, mutations, and innovations.*

What happens when the entire world has access to all the knowledge of the world via the internet for $5 per month? For almost free? What happens when everyone is connected? That shared knowledge network becomes infinitely more powerful and knowledgeable than any single person or node. When that network is powered and assisted by computers and AI, we can expect amazing things to happen.

Pervasive intelligence

Alan Turing was born in London a few years before the Great War, when soldiers still charged into battle wielding swords. It was an interesting time, as technological innovation was beginning to accelerate—those soldiers with swords charged into the missiles of industrial-grade weapons. The first automobiles were roaming streets, and airplanes were new; within about fifty years, men would step foot on the moon. Turing's love of mathematics led him to explore a number of challenging ideas, including the "halting problem," or the question of whether it would be possible to create an algorithm that could determine whether another algorithm would ever complete its operation. Turing's solution was an important step toward the creation of the miraculous devices that power our modern world. Initially computers were thought to be machines that an operator could control. Turing's introduction of programmability and "thinking," of a sort, cracked wide open the notion that the only limit to what computers and programs could ultimately do would be the complexity of the devices. When this idea was carried to its logical conclusion, it became clear that even human imagination might one day no longer be a rate limiter of scientific advancement and innovation.

In 1950, Turing wrote a paper that began, provocatively, with the question, "Can machines think?" "Thinking" is a difficult word to define, so Turing chose to "replace the question by another, which is closely related to it and is expressed in relatively unambiguous words."[3] Turing described the new form of the problem in terms of an "imitation game," in which an interrogator asks questions of a man and a woman in another room to determine the correct sex of the game's players. Turing's remarkable question was, "Are there imaginable digital computers which would do well in the imitation game?" Turing went on to argue in the paper that the answer was yes and that common objections to the proposition that "machines can think" had little or no merit. This "imitation game" became widely known as the "Turing test" and a basis for understanding whether artificial intelligence has been achieved.

The Turing test has been passed. Early versions of large language models (LLMs) are currently in widespread use. Recently, I decided to get creative in tackling the problem of a teenage daughter who was consistently late for morning obligations: I instructed OpenAI's ChatGPT tool to write a poem (in iambic pentameter—why not?) explaining to my daughter why it is important to set an alarm and wake up on time. Nearly instantly, the program returned a well-written poem in rhyming verse that was astonishing for its apparent creativity, depth of understanding of context, and precise language. While the poem ultimately was not persuasive, it did make us laugh and wonder.

OpenAI's ChatGPT is a neural network machine learning model trained using internet data to generate any kind of text. The tool can produce text from practically any prompt with surprisingly humanlike results. Within five days of its release in late 2022, over one million users logged in to experiment with the tool. The internet was quickly awash in examples of AI-generated text, shared by users who were amazed at the sometimes funny, sometimes untrue, and sometimes eerily insightful but frequently surprising results. Entrepreneurs and corporations alike are scrambling to find commercial uses of the technology, which early on is more of an amusing toy than a real productivity booster.

Science fiction author and futurist Arthur C. Clarke once quipped, "Any sufficiently advanced technology is indistinguishable from magic."[4] The output of early LLMs feels like magic to most people. Early LLMs are just the tip of the AI iceberg, as more individuals and organizations begin to explore the ways AI can support content generation, creative tasks, and decision-making. We are just getting started.

In their early form, LLMs write with the organizational skills of a college professor (rigorously structured) but with the reasoning skills of a kindergartner (often wrong). We should expect that to change quickly. Disruptive innovation is a process by which a product or service initially takes root in simple applications, at the low end of the market, before moving upmarket, eventually displacing established solutions. A famous example of disruptive innovation is digital photography: first emerging in the low-end consumer market as a "good enough" alternative to film for consumers who did not like the cost or time involved in film photography, it eventually improved enough to replace analog film cameras in nearly every application, including for high-end professional uses.

Similarly, AI's early state in text and image generation is basic, but it is likely to advance upmarket to disrupt many industries. In the same way that digital photography replaced analog film, AI-generated text will replace human-generated content in many contexts, powering personalized messages in marketing, communications, entertainment, and art.

As AI tools become stronger and more capable, they will present enormous opportunities to businesses of every size. They will also present enormous threats. Every business leader should be nervous and excited about what lies ahead. Every leader of a scaled organization must decide now whether to lead their company into the AI-enabled future or get disrupted by the AI-enabled companies that will take their place. There is no middle ground; most companies will eventually be AI-enabled or extinct.

Leaders should consider how AI-empowered tools can be used to (1) streamline existing operations, (2) improve customer interactions, and (3) create entirely new business models that do not yet exist. Leaders can begin by taking a look at their operations, products, and services and asking,

"What would a smarter version of this look like?" Once leaders know the answer to that question, they should not wait for someone else to build it. That smarter, AI-enabled version is coming if it is not already here, and if leaders are not asking the question and taking control of the solution, their company will not likely be the beneficiary.

Pervasive, AI-enabled computing, coupled with free communications, is going to radically increase the pace of learning required for large corporations to remain competitive. As with any new technology that shows such early promise (like the internet and electrification before it), large corporations should be experimenting with AI through new venture creation (and partnerships, investment, and acquisition, alongside internal R&D).

Run experiments to reassess your operations and customer interactions; build new ventures to explore AI-enabled business models. And do it quickly. Disruptive innovations always lower the cost of access to expertise, and the course of AI will be no different. Soon, individuals and small teams will have access to knowledge and expertise that was previously guarded or hard to unlock. With more access to knowledge and more fluid communication of ideas than ever before in world history, we should expect AI's pace of innovation to be relatively rapid. This revolution will empower individuals and small teams, at the expense of large corporations that are not already in full experimentation mode.

Costless and abundant energy

In 1893, Thomas Edison's young company, General Electric, bid $554,000 to electrify the World's Fair in Chicago using Edison's direct current technology. George Westinghouse claimed he could electrify the fair for only $399,000 using Nikola Tesla's alternating current. Westinghouse won the bid, and the fight between Edison and Westinghouse was on. The ramifications of that battle still impact our lives.

In the same year as the World's Fair, the Niagara Falls Hydraulic Power and Manufacturing Company awarded Westinghouse, with his license for Tesla's AC induction motor patent, the contract to generate electricity from Niagara Falls. Although Tesla's prediction that Niagara Falls could generate enough electricity to power the entire eastern United States did not prove correct, by the end of 1896, the city of Buffalo was powered with alternating current from Niagara Falls. General Electric threw in the towel and decided to adopt alternating current for its generation and distribution. More than a century later, we are still dealing with the benefits and drawbacks of these decisions made in the early days of the electrification race.

Edison developed direct current (called so because it runs continually in a single direction, like a battery). In the early days of electricity, direct current was the standard in the United States. But direct current has a drawback: it's not easily converted to higher or lower voltages.

Tesla believed alternating current was a preferable method. Alternating current reverses direction a certain number of times per second (sixty in the United States) and can be easily converted to higher or lower voltages with a transformer.

Edison and Tesla famously engaged in a war of public relations to discredit the other's preferred technology. Newspaper stories from the 1890s recount tales of hapless individuals who were electrocuted by dangerous current, sometimes while simply walking down the street within too close a range to wire carrying electricity. Not wanting to miss out on royalties from his direct current patents, Edison actively publicized the supposed dangers of alternating current, electrocuting animals with it to prove his point.

When Edison invented the lightbulb, he also had to invent the system to support it: power generation and distribution, metering, wiring, light fixtures, switches, and so on. He had some important choices to make in those early days: Alternating current or direct current? Centralized or distributed generation?

Eventually centralized generation and alternating current became the standard. But in recent years, both distributed generation and direct current have seen a revival. Computers, LEDs, solar cells, and electric vehicles all run on DC power, and technology now exists to convert DC to higher and lower voltages. Direct current is more stable across long transmission distances.

This is a long way to say: none of what we now know as the electric grid had to develop the way it did. The system the world had in 2022 was the result primarily of decisions made over a hundred years before. But whether it's fossil fuel, solar cells, or AC or DC, the power source is ultimately the same: the sun.

Nuclear fusion is the process by which two light atomic nuclei combine to form a single heavier nucleus while releasing massive amounts of energy. Nuclear fusion exists naturally in stars, including our sun, where hydrogen nuclei fuse to create helium while releasing the energy that lights and heats the earth. It is that energy that ultimately is stored in coal, oil, and plants, for example, and converted into electricity.

Research to reproduce fusion power for electricity generation in man-made environments is ongoing and has made dramatic progress in recent years. The technology is still far from commercially viable, but it is marching on a path to that end. Fusion power isn't the only technology that promises to make energy more abundant and cheap. In the meantime, as the price of production drops, it may soon be cheaper to synthesize hydrocarbons from carbon dioxide and water than to drill them out of the ground. As storage technology continues to improve, spikes in energy demand and supply will be better managed, resulting in lower costs. Energy will eventually, and inevitably, be abundant and free. It is a question of when, not if.

Energy superabundance—when it arrives—will change everything. It will drive a revolution in the way humans live. A great deal of fuel is currently used for heating and transportation. With cheap and plentiful electricity we should expect to see more access to transportation, including aviation. Commercial air travel, while safe, is a notoriously buggy and unsatisfying consumer experience. If innovation can deliver cheap and lightweight fuel, it will expand the benefits of global travel to many more people, creating opportunities for more exchange of ideas. Cheap hydrocarbons will revolutionize access to chemicals like plastics, medicine, paints, dyes, and much more. Plentiful energy will remove limitations on the use of heat or mechanical force to move and manipulate objects and on the use of computational power. Abundant energy will limit the negative environmental impact of steel, cement, and other materials and the processes used to manufacture them. Water scarcity will no longer be a problem, as plentiful energy will be used for desalination and other technologies that can produce potable water at scale. Recycling of existing materials will be easier with abundant energy. For many important resources, scarcity will no longer be a challenge. It is remarkable to think about how the world will change and what humans will be able to accomplish.

We have many reasons to be optimistic about the future.

Connecting the dots

Sometime around AD 50, a scientist named Hero of Alexandria (what a name!) published a description of a steam-powered device called an aeolipile. An aeolipile consists of a small receptacle for water with angled outlets to release steam when the water is heated. Below the receptacle, the operator lights a fire, which heats the water, which turns into steam that is released through the angled outlets, causing the receptacle, a basic turbine, to turn.

Hero used a related version of this early steam engine to pull a rope that opened temple doors. With this invention, one might assume the Industrial Revolution was just around the corner. In geologic time spans it was, but it took 1,700 years before James Watt built the first modern steam engine that kicked off the Industrial Revolution.

Over three hundred years after Watt invented his steam engine, engineers at Porsche nearly perfected derivatives of the technology to create an engine that powers the Porsche 911, which if you are lucky, you may have an opportunity to drive on a track at very high speeds.

You can trace the evolution of the technology that powers the modern Porsche back to Hero's invention 2,000 years ago. It took a while—there was a 1,700-year gap between Hero and Watt—and then the evolution started happening faster. The pace of invention accelerated because ideas became easier to exchange—people became more numerous and better connected—and because inventors were able to rely on the building blocks of earlier technologies to create more. It is possible to draw a line from the aeolipile to the modern Porsche, but the line is not straight; it looks more like disconnected dots at some points, and it is more of an exponential curve when it comes to performance.

Exponential curves for linear brains

We are not good at predicting the future because our brains extrapolate in straight lines. Nine weeks before the Wright brothers made their first powered flight, a government-sponsored flight machine failed, and the *New York Times* predicted man wouldn't fly for at least a million years.[5]

As connectedness and the strength of technology building blocks increase, we can expect the pace of innovation to continue accelerating. This means we are on the precipice of massive and rapid change across most fields of invention, change that is exponential and hard to understand.

Futurist Ray Kurzweil explained this phenomenon in what he called the law of accelerating returns, which states that the rate of change in evolutionary systems accelerates over time because of increased access to technology.[6] He didn't say the *amount* of change increases over time—he argued that *the rate* of change actually accelerates. More and better building blocks lead to an acceleration of the pace of change. Change grows exponentially.

Nevertheless, it is hard to be an optimist. Pessimists sound smart. But optimists make money,[7] and they shape the future. Edwin Land, founder of Polaroid and one of the most successful entrepreneurs of the twentieth century, famously argued persuasively that optimism is a moral duty.[8]

You should be an optimist, but for many optimism does not come easy. The problem is that good things take a while, and bad things happen quickly. It is often easier to spot the bad things that happen and harder to notice the good. Progress is sometimes simply the absence of something happening—some bad thing that used to happen like widespread childhood mortality stops happening, and it is not easy to notice in the moment. One must step back and look at the data across long timelines to notice that things are getting better. Additionally, the solutions optimists present usually create new problems! For every answer, there are more questions. Most people these days are pessimistic about the future. Polls show that a majority of people believe things are generally getting worse. This is a new phenomenon.

From enlightenment to pessimism

The eighteenth century was the Age of Enlightenment. Advances in scientific approaches and understanding led people to believe there was no bound to the improvements we could make to our natural environment or the human condition. A French philosopher and mathematician named Nicolas de

Condorcet was the perfect embodiment of this Enlightenment thinking. In *Sketch for a Historical Picture of the Progress of the Human Mind*, he explained how the world was on the verge of a more liberal economy, free and equal public instruction, equality of the sexes and races, and widespread constitutional government. He predicted unlimited steady progress in all domains of human endeavor, forever. Unfortunately (and ironically), he died in prison during the French Revolution.

But the Enlightenment led to widespread hope and optimism. The nineteenth century was considered at the time the Age of Progress. Slavery ended in many parts of the world. It was the beginning of industrialization, and many believed it was the end of toil. There was naive optimism about the future, and in the United States we saw many utopian movements spring up that were representative of the thinking at the time. Around the end of the nineteenth century, Edison said, "I am ashamed at the number of things around my house and shop that are done by [human beings] and ought to be done by a motor without any sense of fatigue or pain. Hereafter a motor must do all the chores."[9] There was a simplistic belief prevalent in the nineteenth century that we were on the precipice of the end of work and toil. As my kids will tell you, chores are still a thing, unfortunately.

And then the twentieth century. One could argue that if the nineteenth century was utopian, the twentieth century was dystopian. Of course, there was tremendous progress on many fronts in the last century, but world wars brought massive death and pain on an industrial scale. The atom bomb was the culmination of scientific discovery but also emblematic of humans' ability to create bigger and deeper problems. People began to wonder, for the first time in hundreds of years, whether progress really was universally constant.

In the last fifty years, possibly until very recently, we actually saw a stagnation of sorts in many fields of invention, including energy, travel, and space. Turning from progress isn't a viable long-term solution, and the pessimism we see in polls currently is not productive, merited, or helpful. We need what author Kevin Kelly has called a protopian, or accurate but also optimistic, view of the future to replace the naivete of earlier centuries and pessimism of the recent past.[10] This isn't to say that progress is inevitable, or that things will get better for everyone from here on out. That is the mistake many utopians made in the past, and it is not an accurate view. Rather, what we should agree on is that on average, things get better over time, and we have reason to believe they will continue to do so. I would go even further and argue that we should expect the pace of improvement to quicken.

Optimism is more likely correct

Optimistic views, on average, over time, have proven more correct than pessimistic views. If you want to be accurate about the future, you are more likely to be right if you are optimistic. Civilization depends on optimism, on the hope and trust that people will generally behave in ways that are predictable. Civilization needs optimists to create the future!

Optimism powers the building of things that endure far beyond our mortal lives and benefit generations to come. My family and I used to live in Massachusetts, down the road from a farm that has been in the same family for over three hundred years. The family possesses the original deed to the land from the king of England, issued back when Massachusetts was still a British colony. Optimism fosters in us a desire to be good ancestors, to build things for our descendants who will come in the future. Cicero talked about the marvel of those who plant trees under whose shade they will never sit.

Optimism bestows resilience and adaptability. If being optimistic is the correct view, on average, over time, then being optimistic—but also realistic—will help us be better prepared for the future that is to come. It is a fallacy to think that pessimists are better prepared. Pessimists are more likely to be caught off guard.

Optimists shape the future, and you should want to shape the future.

There has never been a better time, on average, to be alive. This is an optimistic statement to put in print, where it will remain static but also likely true, no matter who is reading this and when.

Poverty and violence have sharply decreased over the last several decades. Life expectancies have increased, as have rates of freedom and democracy across the globe. Although sometimes it seems hard to believe, we work fewer hours, on average, than we did in the middle of the twentieth century. You are less likely to die on an airplane, less likely to die in a car, less likely to be killed on the job, and less likely to die in a natural disaster than your grandparents. Violence is down dramatically from historic levels, poverty has decreased precipitously over the last few decades, and food production is incredibly more efficient than it used to be. According to many measures, the world is getting better and the human condition is improving, strikingly so.

That does not mean there are not big problems—there are enormous problems yet to solve, and there always will be— but on average, the realistic view is that things are getting much, much better, and our capacity to develop solutions to new problems will continue to increase.

While we have seen some stagnation over the last few decades in some areas of technology (e.g., we fly in the same airplanes, more or less, that we flew in sixty years ago), we have seen massive improvements in others (e.g., information technology). Many believe the "Great Stagnation" that economist and polymath Tyler Cowen described in his book of that title may be coming to an end. Either way, across long time spans, a decades-long slowdown in a technology segment is a blip; the trend continues over time to move up and to the right.

Living within exponential growth curves

When you're in the middle of the action, it is hard to perceive exponential growth curves. We extrapolate in straight lines; our brains process linearly. We rely on past growth rates to project the future; but what happens when growth rates are actually accelerating, as Kurzweil predicts? The trajectory of recent history tells us a distorted story. Progress isn't smooth; there are dips and cycles. But when you zoom out, those dips are mere squiggles on an exponential curve. An example: The World Bank tracks gross world product per capita. This is a hard number to calculate, so there are likely some errors in the data, but the results over the years are probably directionally correct.

World GDP Over the Last Two Millennia

Total output of the world economy. This data is adjusted for inflation and differences in the cost of living between countries

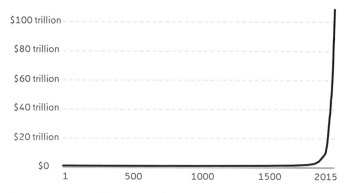

Data source: Our World in Data based on World Bank & Maddison (2017), OurWorldInData.org/economic-growth | CC BY. Note: This data is expressed in international-$[1] at 2011 prices.

Since 1960, gross world product has increased about 5 percent per year. A remarkable run. If you apply the same growth rate over the next fifty years, things get crazy, and we're just at the start. This assumes the growth rate holds steady *and doesn't increase.* We can't predict with certainty what will happen, but we know that the run since 1960 has been incredible, and there is no reason to believe the trends that fueled that growth are abating. It is hard to perceive the change when you're in the middle of it.

Another example: The amount of venture capital invested in the United States grew at close to 20 percent annually, on average, from 2007 to 2022. There were dips in the trendline, of course, and no one knows if that growth rate of venture capital will continue; many things would need to be true for this to happen. Given how small venture capital is in the universe of investable assets relative to its impact, there are plenty of reasons to believe the growth rate will continue. If one assumes a steady growth rate for the next twenty years, the upward curve looks dramatic—like the proverbial hockey stick. Whether you agree with the trend or not—and if you want to, assume a steady growth rate that is much smaller than we have seen over the last decade—the numbers look likely to get very big, very quickly. The question I ask when I see this is: Where will all the companies come from? There will be demand for many more companies than we're creating today. It's time to start building!

A final example: Author Holden Karnofsky has mapped out a timeline showing the increasing pace of innovation since the start of human civilization.[11] Whether artificial general intelligence and other breakthrough advancements come in the next one hundred years or the next five hundred is inconsequential in the grand scheme of things. It's all a blip on the chart. The point is we are currently living right at that unique moment in the history of the universe when things go crazy and exponential. It is an amazing and meaningful time to be alive. What you do about it now can matter quite a lot.

If you stand back and look at technology developments that have occurred just in the last twelve or twenty-four months (no matter when you read this), you will likely be amazed at the progress, much of which is otherwise hard to notice in the day-to-day march of bad news. The next one hundred years will surely be even more amazing and weird, in the aggregate. At a minimum, looking at historical trends, it is safe to assume that the progress of the next twenty-five years will exceed the progress of the last twenty-five.

Be contrarian and right

Despite that, it feels somewhat contrarian to be an optimist. The data tells us we should be optimistic. There is an amazing opportunity in front of all of us who are optimistic about the future, thinking in long horizons, and actively working to build the future; it is a chance to be contrarian and right, and to earn big rewards (however you define them) because of it.

How should you act differently with this knowledge from those around you who are not as optimistic? A few ideas:

- First, think about ways you might use time horizons as a competitive advantage. Play to the long-term curve, not the dips. Amazon is famously a company that uses time horizons as a competitive advantage. What that means is that they have organized the company *to be able to wait longer than their competition*. How might you organize your organization around longer timelines? One way to do that is to focus on optimizing for resilience over efficiency. This means more small bets and experiments, more balance sheet investment, more learning, and generally doing things to create more optionality.

- Recognize that new solutions will lead to new problems that need to be solved. Anticipate and solve future problems and worry less about current ones. Develop a hypothesis about the future and make it happen. March in that direction, and stay true. Entrepreneurs organize around optimistic hypotheses about the future, the accelerating pace of innovation, increased opportunities to build, and the shift in power from large institutions to individuals and small teams.

- Your ideas about the future—and the products, projects, and businesses you're working on—are likely not weird enough. If you're seeing innovation in the market that looks strange—crypto and NFTs are recent examples that have generated widespread experimentation—do not dismiss them out of hand. Seek to understand. What do others believe that you do not? What bets are they making? Why are weird ideas taking hold and what do they tell us about future opportunities? Seek and embrace surprises, and take action to create the data you need to move further.

- Finally, play to win—do not play not to lose. This requires making bets and choosing controversial strategies. Playing it safe *ensures* you will lose. Play offense. In the world of venture building and investment, we often think in terms of a 2 × 2 where the axes are consensus/

nonconsensus and right/wrong. There are few, if any, rewards waiting for those who are right and follow the consensus. The big rewards are available to those who are contrarian, who make nonconsensus bets and end up being right.

Rewards Go to Those Who Are Contrarian and Correct

	WRONG	RIGHT
CONSENSUS	X	$
NON CONSENSUS	X	$$$

Optimism is not ignorance of problems. There are many problems. *Every solution creates more problems, and every answer more questions.* Optimism is understanding the good news that our capacity to solve problems can increase. In the coming age of abundance—an age that we are arguably already living in—when communications, computing, and power are free, innovation will move incredibly quickly. Large organizations will rise and die much faster, at incredible cost, if they do not learn how to take advantage of the trends and manufacture serendipity through faster cycles of experimentation.

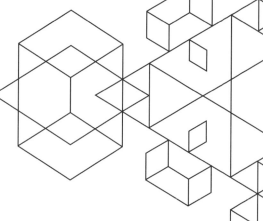

12

Conclusion

Change is hard, but not changing
is much harder.

Years ago a multinational automobile manufacturer sent me and a small team to India to help them improve their operations and define their strategy. At the time, the company was losing $1 million per day in that market.

Our task was twofold: (1) stop the bleeding by defining a more realistic near-term strategy for the existing business and (2) figure out a long-term strategy to profit from future, technology-enabled changes to "mobility." Figuring out what kinds of opportunities technology would enable in the future was fun and relatively easy. My team and I spent months traveling around India, interviewing consumers and other market participants to understand their needs: we met with the poorest of the poor and the richest of the rich in more than twelve cities around the country. In the end, we interviewed over one hundred people and came away with strong hypotheses about how software and sensors would impact traffic management, how to solve "last mile" logistical problems, and how to apply disruptive innovation theory to serve the "low end" of the market and get footholds that would enable the company to march upmarket over time.

None of that would ever be possible if the company couldn't solve its near-term challenges, however. And that problem proved to be very tricky.

During my travels around the country, I met with an impressive entrepreneur, Jagdish Khattar, who played an instrumental role in building and running one of the most successful automobile manufacturers in India, called Maruti Suzuki. (The company was built in partnership with the Japanese manufacturer, Suzuki.) Khattar was obsessed with keeping costs low so he could sell vehicles profitably in a market where per capita income is relatively low, if rising. Most of the parts that went into Maruti Suzuki's vehicles were manufactured in India. In contrast, the multinational corporation I was working with had global supply chains that brought parts from many markets where operating expenses were significantly higher. When I met Khattar for lunch, he handed me his business card, which was clearly made by hand. His secretary created "cards" on a sheet of paper that she printed in the office and cut with scissors. The edges and angles were imperfect, but the message was clear: this is a company that keeps costs low. When I saw this business card, I knew immediately that the multinational company I was working with would never be able to compete with Maruti Suzuki on cost.

I took the business card with me to my next meeting at the multinational's Asia headquarters in Shanghai and showed the card to some executives as an example of what they were dealing with in India. "Until you're ready to print and cut your own business cards," I told them, "you're going to have trouble competing with this company on cost."

My team and I showed them a chart we had made that tracked the price of Maruti Suzuki's base model over time. In the decade or more that the car had been on the market, its inflation-adjusted price had declined each year, while features and quality had steadily increased. The chart showed, improbably, that without a change in the pricing trend, within twelve years Maruti Suzuki would somehow be able to sell a high-quality vehicle to consumers for free.

Our recommendation to the multinational? Stop making cars in India, specialize in SUVs, and focus on future mobility opportunities. Not an easy recommendation to accept for automotive executives who *love* making cars.

I delivered the recommendation to the CEO and other top executives in a crowded conference room in Shanghai. I remember going through the argument in exquisite detail, using the data we had collected through extensive research and interviews. I laid out a range of strategic alternatives for the short term that involved everything from partnership to acquisition to market exit, but each option depended on the company stopping the manufacture of automobiles. The executives nodded their heads knowingly: the data was hard to argue with, and the status quo path ahead looked difficult. No decision was expected in that meeting; it was going to take time to wrestle with the implications. I couldn't tell right away whether they found my argument persuasive. (Spoiler alert: they did not find my argument persuasive, at least not immediately.)

After I finished my presentation, I sat down in the back of the room to watch the next speaker, an executive from the India operation, who had brought design renderings for the side mirrors for a vehicle model the company was planning to launch in the Indian market the following year. The executives—all passionate about cars and their designs—sat on the edge of their seats and became animated by the discussion about the intricacies and options related to the side mirror design. They couldn't wait for the new model to come out. Even though we had just discussed how each vehicle they sold would surely lose money.

The multinational automobile manufacturer exited the Indian market eventually, but it took much longer than it should have.

Change is hard. But not changing is much harder.

It is difficult to steer a scaled organization in a new direction. Incentives for safety, predictability, and risk eradication are tenacious. Entrenched incentives and metrics seem logical because they explain how the world worked in the past. Abandoning them feels dangerous.

Because organizations are better managed than ever for safety and predictability, organizations have become less capable of adapting to changing times. But change is coming, whether corporations want it or not. The future is approaching very quickly, and it's going to be much weirder than we can imagine. The solutions we develop along the way to existing problems will only create new problems to solve, and some of those problems will be so big and complex that only scaled organizations will be capable of addressing them.

We need our scaled institutions, including corporations, to be better at solving big problems again. This means questioning decades of embedded assumptions about why corporations exist and finding ways to empower small teams—through better incentives—to conduct more of the experiments we need: faster, weirder, and cheaper. It's time to build. The future is not predetermined, and we all have a role to play in its direction.

Acknowledgments

Ginger Parker, for everything

David and Lauren Parker, for encouraging a love of business, history, and learning

Bret Swanson, for his collaboration in 2018 that planted the seed for some of the chapters in this book

Clayton Christensen, for his mentorship and world-changing ideas that have been a foundation to my career and this book

John Garry, for reading an early version of the manuscript and providing insightful feedback

Ken Stanley, for opening my eyes about how to accomplish big things

Lauren Kellum, for applying her world-class organization and design skills to everything she does

Matt Rubin, for helping arrange the contents of my first draft

Ryan Larcom, for injecting ideas to reinforce key concepts in the book

The entire team at High Alpha Innovation, who are working to shepherd corporations into a more decentralized future through the co-creation of amazing, advantaged startups

Endnotes

Chapter 1

1 Emily Langer, "Gerald Shur, Founder of the Federal Witness Protection Program, Dies at 86," *Washington Post*, 7 September 2020, www.washingtonpost.com/local/obituaries/gerald-shur-founder-of-the-federal-witness-protection-program-dies-at-86/2020/09/02/6fe09696-eba5-11ea-b4bc-3a2098fc73d4_story.html.

2 Clayton M. Christensen, *The Innovator's Dilemma: When New Technologies Cause Great Firms to Fail* (Boston: Harvard Business Review Press, 2016).

3 Clayton M. Christensen, "A Capitalist's Dilemma, Whoever Wins on Tuesday," *New York Times*, 3 November 2012, https://www.nytimes.com/2012/11/04/business/a-capitalists-dilemma-whoever-becomes-president.html.

4 Clayton M. Christensen and Derek van Bever, "The Capitalist's Dilemma," *Harvard Business Review*, June 2014, hbr.org/2014/06/the-capitalists-dilemma.

5 "Nonfinancial Corporate Business; Liquid Assets (Broad Measure), Level." FRED Economic Data, 8 June 2023, fred.stlouisfed.org/series/BOGZ1FL104001005Q.

6   Ibid.

7   Ezra Klein, "Francis Fukuyama: America Is in 'One of the Most Severe Political Crises I Have Experienced,'" Vox, 26 October 2016, www.vox. com/2016/10/26/13352946/francis-fukuyama-ezra-klein.

8   David Ogilvy, *Ogilvy on Advertising*, (United Kingdom: Welbeck Publishing, 2023).

Chapter 2

1   Valeo, "Acceleration in Outperformance and Cash Generation in 2019," Valeo, 20 February 2020, www.valeo.com/wp-content/uploads/2020/02/press_release_2019_results_en.pdf.

2   Joe Miller et al. "Weakest Link in Supply Chain Threatens Car Industry Revival," *Financial Times*, 16 April 2020, www.ft.com/content/9d3b2243-5e26-4890-918f-ec1daee33ffb.

3   Carly Graf, "Van Ness Avenue BRT to Finally Begin Service Early Next Year," *San Francisco Examiner*, 24 April 2021, www.sfexaminer. com/archives/van-ness-avenue-brt-to-finally-begin-service-early-next-year/article_3a00ec97-cfab-5b18-b379-5b32c6cee006.html.

4   US Department of Transportation, "Alaska Highway," Federal Highway Administration, Accessed 10 August 2023, www.fhwa.dot.gov/candc/factsheets/alaskahighway.pdf; "Alaska Highway," Bell Travel Guides, Accessed 19 June 2023, www.bellsalaska.com/highway/alaska-highway/; "Inflation Calculator," CPI Inflation Calculator, Accessed 10 August 2023, www.in2013dollars.com/us/inflation/.

Chapter 3

1   Reed Hastings and Ben Horowitz, "Designing a Culture of Reinvention," *A16Z Podcast*, 2 June 2022, a16z.com/2020/09/15/a16z-podcast-designing-a-culture-of-reinvention/.

2   Michael J. Mauboussin and Kristen Bartholdson, "The Babe Ruth Effect," *Consilient Observer*, 29 January 2002, www.pmjar.com/wp-content/uploads/2014/03/The-Babe-Ruth-Effect-Frequency-versus-Magnitude1.pdf.

3   Clayton Christensen (@claychristensen). 2016. "The worst place to develop a new business model is from within your existing business model." Twitter, 9 February 2016, 11:53AM. twitter.com/claychristensen/status/697101123031793665.

Chapter 4

1   Jerry Hausman et al. "The Effects of the Breakup of AT&T on Telephone Penetration in the United States," *American Economic Review*, vol. 83, no. 2 (May 1993): 178–84. *JSTOR*, http://www.jstor.org/stable/2117661.

2   In the early 20th century, for example, a private militia controlled by the Cuyamel Fruit Company deposed and replaced the president of Honduras. In 1904, the American author O. Henry coined the term "banana republic" to describe countries exploited by militarized corporations.

3   Raymond M. Wolfe, "Businesses Reported an 11.8% Increase to Nearly a Half Trillion Dollars for US R&D Performance during 2019," National Center for Science and Engineering Statistics, 18 November 2021, ncses.nsf.gov/pubs/nsf22303.

4   Patrick Collison and Michael Nielsen, "Science Is Getting Less Bang for Its Buck," *The Atlantic*, 28 November 2018, www.theatlantic.com/science/archive/2018/11/diminishing-returns-science/575665/.

5   Nicholas Bloom et al. "Are Ideas Getting Harder to Find?," National Bureau of Economic Research, September 2017, www.nber.org/system/files/working_papers/w23782/w23782.pdf.

6   Ibid.

7   Sirio Aramonte, "Mind the Buybacks, Beware of the Leverage," The Bank for International Settlements, 14 September 2020, www.bis.org/publ/qtrpdf/r_qt2009d.htm.

8   "S&P 500 Q4 2022 Buybacks Tick Up, as 2022 Sets a Record; Proforma Buyback Tax Would Have Reduced Operating Earnings by 0.51% for 2022," S&P Global, 21 March 2023, press.spglobal.com/2023-03-21-

S-P-500-Q4-2022-Buybacks-Tick-up,-As-2022-Sets-A-Record-Profor-ma-Buyback-Tax-Would-Have-Reduced-Operating-Earnings-by-0-51-for-2022/.

9   Dorothy Neufeld, "Charted: The Rise of Stock Buybacks over 20 Years," *Visual Capitalist*, 1 December 2022, advisor.visualcapitalist.com/rise-of-stock-buybacks/.

10 S. Patrick Viguerie et al. "2021 Corporate Longevity Forecast," Innosight Strategy and Innovation at Huron, May 2021, www.innosight.com/insight/creative-destruction/.

11 Michael J. Mauboussin and Dan Callahan, "Counterpoint Global Insights: Birth, Death, and Wealth Creation," *Consilient Observer*, Morgan Stanley, 25 July 2023, www.morganstanley.com/im/publication/insights/articles/article_birthdeathandwealthcreation.pdf?1690283806853.

12 "At a Glance: FactSet Mergers Datafeed," FactSet, 3 October 2019, insight.factset.com/resources/factset-mergers-datafeed.

Chapter 5

1   Sarah Frier, "The Inside Story of How Facebook Acquired Instagram," Medium, 5 August 2020, onezero.medium.com/the-inside-story-of-how-facebook-acquired-instagram-318f244f1283.

2   Packy McCormick, "Compounding Crazy," Not Boring by Packy McCormick, 2 August 2021, www.notboring.co/p/compounding-crazy.

3   Sungki Hong and Devin Werner, "How Many People Does It Take to Start a Company?," Federal Reserve Bank of St. Louis, 9 July 2020, www.stlouisfed.org/publications/regional-economist/second-quarter-2020/many-people-does-it-take-start-company.

4   Peter A. Thiel and Blake G. Masters, *Zero to One: Notes on Startups, or How to Build the Future* (United Kingdom: Ebury Publishing, 2014).

5   Daron Acemoglu et al. "Innovation, Reallocation, and Growth." Becker Friedman Institute for Economics at the University of Chicago, November 2017, https://bfi.uchicago.edu/wp-content/uploads/WP_2017-21.pdf.

6   Ufuk Akcigit and Nathan Goldschlag, "Where Have All the 'Creative Talents' Gone? Employment Dynamics of US Inventors," National Bureau of Economic Research, 25 March 2023, static1.squarespace. com/static/57fa873e8419c230ca01eb5f/t/641f8c63b35c6d1cb1c-76de7/1679789155771/Akcigit_Goldschlag_Talent_NBER.pdf.

7   Office of Advocacy, "Small Business Facts: Small Business Job Creation," US Small Business Administration Office of Advocacy, 26 April 2022, advocacy.sba.gov/2022/04/26/small-business-facts-small-business-job-creation/.

8   Marc Andreessen, "Why Software Is Eating the World," Andreessen Horowitz, 20 August 2011, a16z.com/2011/08/20/why-software-is-eating-the-world/.

Chapter 6

1   "The Amazon and Water," Amazon Aid Foundation, 21 June 2020, amazonaid.org/resources/about-the-amazon/the-amazon-and-water/.

2   Fred Pearce, "Weather Makers," *Science*, 18 June 2020, www.science. org/content/article/controversial-russian-theory-claims-forests-don-t-just-make-rain-they-make-wind.

3   Jerry Coyne, "The Peppered Moth Story Is Solid," *Why Evolution Is True*, 10 February 2012, whyevolutionistrue.com/2012/02/10/the-peppered-moth-story-is-solid/.

4   Andreas Wagner, *Life Finds a Way: What Evolution Teaches Us about Creativity* (New York: Basic Books, 2019).

5   Colin Bryar and Bill Carr, "Organizing: Separable, Single-Threaded Leadership," *Working Backwards: Insights, Stories, and Secrets from Inside Amazon* (New York: St. Martin's Press, 2021).

6   A robust defense of this idea can be found in *Why Greatness Cannot Be Planned: The Myth of the Objective* by Kenneth O. Stanley and Joel Lehman (Switzerland: Springer, 2015).

Chapter 7

1   Elizabeth Weil, "They Know How to Prevent Megafires. Why Won't Anybody Listen?," *ProPublica*, 28 August 2020, www.propublica.org/article/they-know-how-to-prevent-megafires-why-wont-anybody-listen.

2   "California Forest Carbon Plan," California Natural Resources Agency, May 2018, resources.ca.gov/CNRALegacyFiles/wp-content/uploads/2018/05/California-Forest-Carbon-Plan-Final-Draft-for-Public-Release-May-2018.pdf.

Chapter 8

1   Gary A. Klein, *Seeing What Others Don't: The Remarkable Ways We Gain Insights* (New York: PublicAffairs, 2013).

2   "Unicorn" is a company that achieves a $1 billion or greater exit.

3   Eduardo M. Azevedo et al. "A/B Testing with Fat Tails." Github Pages, 9 August 2019, eduardomazevedo.github.io/papers/azevedo-et-al-ab.pdf.

4   James Clear, "The Shadow Side of Greatness," James Clear, 3 February 2020, jamesclear.com/shadow-side.

5   "List of Compositions by Johann Sebastian Bach," Wikipedia, 21 August 2023, en.wikipedia.org/wiki/List_of_compositions_by_Johann_Sebastian_Bach.

6   Edmund Morris, *Edison* (New York: Random House, 2019).

7   Neal Gabler, *Walt Disney: The Triumph of the American Imagination* (New York: Alfred A. Knopf, 2006).

8   Ibid.

9   Ibid.

10 Ibid.

11 Kenneth O. Stanley and Joel Lehman, *Why Greatness Cannot Be Planned: The Myth of the Objective* (Switzerland: Springer, 2015).

12 Ibid.

13 Ibid.

14 Andrew Carnegie, *The Autobiography of Andrew Carnegie and the Gospel of Wealth* (New York: Signet Classics, 2006).

15 Ibid.

16 Ibid.

17 Ibid.

Chapter 9

1 David DuPree, "New Twist in NBA: The 3-Point Goal," *Washington Post*, 11 October 1979, www.washingtonpost.com/archive/sports/1979/10/11/new-twist-in-nba-the-3-point-goal/e5547a77-ec79-491c-af8e-b09966d893a6/.

2 "Fred Brown (Basketball)," Wikipedia, 9 July 2023, en.wikipedia.org/wiki/Fred_Brown_(basketball).

3 David DuPree, "New Twist in NBA: The 3-Point Goal," *Washington Post*, 11 October 1979, www.washingtonpost.com/archive/sports/1979/10/11/new-twist-in-nba-the-3-point-goal/e5547a77-ec79-491c-af8e-b09966d893a6/.

4 John Schuhmann, "NBA's 3-Point Revolution: How 1 Shot Is Changing the Game," NBA.Com, 14 October 2021, www.nba.com/news/3-point-era-nba-75.

5 Ibid.

6 Kirk Goldsberry, "How Mapping Shots in the NBA Changed It Forever," FiveThirtyEight, 2 May 2019, fivethirtyeight.com/features/how-mapping-shots-in-the-nba-changed-it-forever/.

7 Sebastien Darius, "Basketball Analytics, Part 2: Shot Quality," Medium, 16 July 2021, towardsdatascience.com/part-2-shot-quality-5ab27fd-63f5e.

8 Ben Cohen, "The One Number That Explains the NBA's 3-Point Revolution," *Wall Street Journal*, 21 Jan. 2021, www.wsj.com/articles/nba-3-point-revolution-11611190418.

9   For a deeper exploration on this idea, see Michael Mankins and Mark Gottfredson. "Strategy-Making in Turbulent Times," *Harvard Business Review*, 16 August 2022, hbr.org/2022/09/strategy-making-in-turbulent-times.

Chapter 10

1   S. Patrick Viguerie et al. "2021 Corporate Longevity Forecast," Innosight Strategy and Innovation at Huron, May 2021, www.innosight.com/insight/creative-destruction/.

2   Hendrik (Hank) Bessembinder, "Shareholder Wealth Enhancement, 1926 to 2022," SSRN, Elsevier, June 17, 2023, https://ssrn.com/abstract=4448099.

3   Paul Kedrosky, "The Constant: Companies That Matter," Ewing Marion Kauffman Foundation, May 2013, www.kauffman.org/wp-content/uploads/2019/12/companiesthatmatter.pdf.

4   James Olan Hutcheson, "The End of a 1,400-Year-Old Business," *Bloomberg.com*, 16 April 2007, web.archive.org/web/20160311042613/www.bloomberg.com:80/news/articles/2007-04-16/the-end-of-a-1-400-year-old-businessbusinessweek-business-news-stock-market-and-financial-advice.

5   James Carse, *Finite and Infinite Games* (New York: Free Press, 2012).

6   "5 Ways Oxford University Has Changed in the Past Century (and 2 Ways It Will Change in the Future)," Oxford Royale Academy, 16 March 2021, www.oxford-royale.com/articles/oxford-university-changes/.

7   John D. Rockefeller, *The 38 Letters from J.D. Rockefeller to His Son: Perspectives, Ideology, and Wisdom* (OpenStax, 2023).

8   Long Now Foundation, "Continuity: Discovering the Lessons Behind the World's Longest-Lived Organizations," YouTube, 25:47, 29 April 2021, https://youtu.be/gmdnCyM8y-s?si=_asnuup62hnQh82V. Accessed 22 Oct. 2023.

9   "The Top 12 Reasons Startups Fail," CB Insights, 3 August 2021, www.cbinsights.com/research/report/startup-failure-reasons-top/.

10 Paul Graham, "Be Good," Paul Graham, April 2008, www.paulgraham.com/good.html.

11 Dominic Rushe, "Jeff Bezos Tells Employees 'One Day Amazon Will Fail,'" *Guardian*, 16 November 2018, www.theguardian.com/technology/2018/nov/16/jeff-bezos-amazon-will-fail-recording-report.

12 Jeff Bezos, "2008 Letter to Shareholders," US Securities and Exchange Commission, April 2009, www.sec.gov/Archives/edgar/data/1018724/000119312509081096/dex991.htm.

Chapter 11

1   Tim Urban, "The AI Revolution: The Road to Superintelligence," Wait But Why, 22 January 2015, https://waitbutwhy.com/2015/01/artificial-intelligence-revolution-1.html.

2   William D. Nordhaus, "Do Real-Output and Real-Wage Measures Capture Reality? The History of Lighting Suggests Not," in *The Economics of New Goods*, ed. Timothy F. Bresnahan and Robert J. Gordon (Chicago: University of Chicago Press, 1996), 27–70. National Bureau of Economic Research, Accessed 3 November 2023, https://www.nber.org/system/files/chapters/c6064/c6064.pdf.

3   Alan M. Turing, "Computing Machinery and Intelligence," *Mind* 59, no. 236 (October 1950): 433–60, https://academic.oup.com/mind/article/LIX/236/433/986238.

4   Arthur C. Clarke, *Profiles of the Future* (London: Indigo, 2000).

5   "Flying Machines Which Do Not Fly," *New York Times*, 9 October 1903, https://www.nytimes.com/1903/10/09/archives/flying-machines-which-do-not-fly.html.

6   Ray Kurzweil, "The Law of Accelerating Returns," The Kurzweil Library, 7 March 2001, www.thekurzweillibrary.com/the-law-of-accelerating-returns.

7   Patrick Collison (@patrickc). 2020. "'Pessimists sound smart. Optimists make money.' —@natfriedman." Twitter, 21 May 2020, 10:52AM. twitter.com/patrickc/status/1263482890668503041.

8   Dan Cordtz, "How Polaroid Bet Its Future on the SX-70," *Fortune Magazine*, January 1974. OpenSX70, 21 January 2021, opensx70.com/posts/2021/01/bet.

9   "The Utilization of Electrical Force," *Rural Californian*, vol. 34, The Kruckeberg Press, 1910.

10 Kevin Kelly, "Protopia," *Technium*, accessed 13 August 2023, kk.org/thetechnium/protopia/.

11 Holden Karnofsky, "The 'Most Important Century' Blog Post Series," Cold Takes, accessed 31 July 2023, www.cold-takes.com/most-important-century/.

Index

Note: Endnote information is denoted by *n* and note number following the page number.